ray
bradbury

Recognitions

detective/suspense · science fiction

Dick Riley, General Editor

Critical Encounters: Writers and Themes in Science Fiction, edited by Dick Riley
Ross Macdonald by Jerry Speir
Sons of Sam Spade: The Private-Eye Novel in the 70s by David Geherin

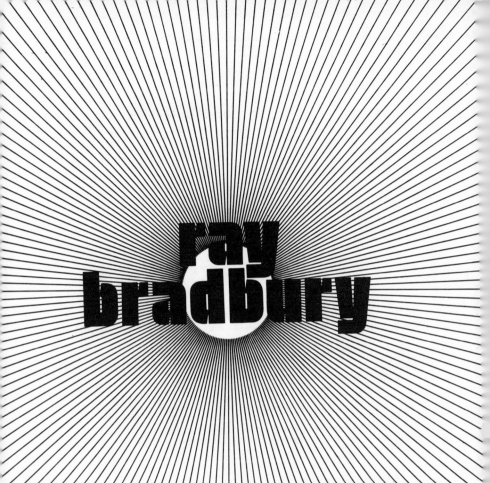

ray bradbury

Wayne L. Johnson

FREDERICK UNGAR PUBLISHING CO. NEW YORK

Library of Congress Cataloging in Publication Data

Johnson, Wayne L. 1942–
  Ray Bradbury.

  Bibliography: p.
  Includes index.
  1. Bradbury, Ray, 1920–   —Criticism and
interpretation.

PS3503.R167Z72   813'.54   79-4825
ISBN 0-8044-2426-8
ISBN 0-8044-6318-2 (pbk.)

Book Design by Marsha Picker

for my mother and father

contents

preface

■ This is a book about a dreamer. Ray Bradbury is a writer with a particular skill at committing his dreams to paper and, in so doing, making them live for others. He dreams dreams of magic and transformation, good and evil, small-town America and the canals of Mars. His dreams are not only popular—they are durable. The great body of his work consists of short stories, which are notoriously difficult to publish and keep before the public eye. Yet his stories have stayed in print, in some cases for nearly three decades.

The subjects that engage Bradbury's pen are many: magic, horror, and monsters; rockets, robots, time and space travel; growing up in a midwestern town in the 1920s, and growing old in an abandoned earth colony on another planet. Despite their varied themes, Bradbury's stories contain a sense of wonder, often a sense of joy, and a lyrical and rhythmic touch that sets his work apart.

Using an analytical approach to such stories is to do a kind of violence to them, but between the dream and the finished story is a considerable amount of craftsmanship. The illustration of that craftsmanship, along with some elucidation of the writer's themes, hopefully will enrich the reader's understanding and appreciation of one of the major artists in his field.

The approach here is thematic: the various collections of Bradbury's stories have been "taken apart," and the stories regrouped and compared with one another in terms of elements and common themes.

Generally speaking, Bradbury's handling of a given theme in an early story as compared to a later story is essentially the same. That is, his themes do not display a growth in emotional depth or logical complexity as time goes on. Instead, Bradbury treats his themes in what might be called a Baroque manner—changing the ornamentation, emotional tone, or relative prominence of the theme from story to story. In a way, this is like the variations on a theme in music. For example, "The Next in Line" and "The Life Work of Juan Diaz" both center around the mummies in the cemetery at Guanajuato in Mexico. The former is a horror story as well as a psychological study of a marital relationship. The latter describes a very different marital relationship and concludes on a note of whimsical irony. Both stories may be compared in terms of the mummies or in the larger context of Bradbury's visit to Mexico in 1945. But little understanding is added from a critical standpoint in knowing that "The Next in Line" was published in 1947 and "The Life work of Juan Diaz" in 1963. For the purposes of this study, then, the order in which the stories were written or published has been largely ignored. Readers wishing to pursue a chronological study of a given theme or themes will want to consult the helpful chronology compiled by William F. Nolan for the 1973 Doubleday & Co., Inc. edition of *The Martian Chronicles.*

As a practical matter, consideration here is limited primarily to fiction available to the general reader. Though this qualification includes the vast bulk of Bradbury's output, certain stories not included in the major collections, as well as Bradbury's nonfiction, are either not mentioned at all, or given brief attention where relevant. Bradbury's poetry, plays, screenplays, and children's books are touched upon in the last chapter, especially as they involve themes covered elsewhere in this book.

I have referred above to Bradbury as being one of the major artists in his field. It should be understood at the outset that there is a considerable amount of confusion as to just what this field is. The demands of the commercial marketplace and the need to confine a popular writer and his work within an easily recognizable image have resulted in Bradbury's being jammed uncomfortably into the box labeled "Science Fiction." No definition of science fiction exists that pleases every body, and even if it did, to apply it casually to the work of Ray Bradbury would be inaccurate and unfair. H. G. Wells, whom many regard as a classic science fiction writer, had this to say about his own novels: "They are all fantasies; they do not aim to project a serious possibility; they aim indeed only at the same amount of conviction as one gets in a good gripping dream. They have to hold the reader to the end by art and illusion and not by proof and argument, and the moment he closes the cover and reflects he wakes up to their impossibility." Wells here is contrasting his stories with those of Jules Verne, which he calls "anticipatory inventions." Viewed this way, virtually all of Bradbury's stories are fantasies, with Wells's concept of the "good gripping dream" coming closest to describing their effect.

Bradbury's first publishing successes were in the pages of the horror, detective, and science fiction pulp magazines of the '40s. As a result, his work has suffered from a certain amount of guilt by association with these forms of popular literature. When in the 1950s Bradbury began to publish regularly in major "slick" magazines, he was often referred to as having broken out of the limited field of science fiction. But this was not due so much to a change on Bradbury's part as to a recognition of the quality of his writing by a larger audience. Even today, Bradbury's place in literature is far from clear. On one hand, Harlan Ellison cites him as an example of how good science fiction can be: "Every time we try to hype some nonbeliever into accepting sf and fantasy as legitimate *literature,* we refer him or her to the words of Ray Bradbury. . . . We whirl them over to the meager sf racks in most bookstores and we may find no Delany, no Lafferty, no Knight or Disch or Dickson, but by God, we always find *The Martian Chronicles.*" On the other hand, Clifton Fadiman, in his prefatory note to the 1954 Bantam edition of *The Martian Chronicles,* seems a bit condescending in noting that the book ". . . has lifted itself easily out of the ruck of its competitors," and in calling Bradbury a "moralist." True as these assertions may be, they reflect common attempts to reassure the insecure reader that Bradbury's writing is somehow worthwhile, and therefore all right to take seriously—reassurances which Bradbury neither seeks nor requires. Bradbury regards himself as an entertainer, more specifically a magician, and his stories are written primarily to amuse. Perhaps the passage of time will alleviate the problem of which niche Bradbury is to occupy—or better still, subvert the tendency to pigeonhole him all together. Few today would insist on labeling Rudyard Kipling an "Indian" writer, or feel it necessary to apologize for enjoying the entertainments of Saki (H. H. Munro). In a somewhat similar fashion, Bradbury's literary family goes beyond the Arthur C. Clarkes and the Isaac Asimovs, to include such recorders of small-town America as Sinclair Lewis and Sherwood Anderson, and such contemporary fantasists as Roald Dahl and John Collier.

I am particularly grateful to Ray Bradbury for taking time out from a very busy schedule to grant me an interview, and for answering my barrage of questions with such enthusiasm. The following individuals were kind enough to supply information on several aspects of "Green Town" from their respective areas of expertise: on rail service, Tom Judge of the Chicago and North Western Transportation Co.; on the trolley, Jim Foley of the Illinois Railway Museum; on the ravine, Dr. L. L. Sloss of the Department of Geology, Northwestern University. This book owes much to the continued support and encouragement of Yvette Tetrault, to the editorial supervision of Dick Riley, and to the competent manuscript typing of Bill Williams. Finally, for their kind assistance to a stranger in town, I would like to thank Diane Taylor in Waukegan, and John and Gail Kahan in Los Angeles.

W.L.J.
Chicago, Illinois

1

the writer and his work

■ Ray Bradbury was born August 22, 1920 in the small town of Waukegan, Illinois, to Leonard Spaulding and Esther Moberg Bradbury. Esther Bradbury was a great film buff (Bradbury's middle name is Douglas, after Douglas Fairbanks), and she passed her enthusiasm on to her son. "My mother took me to see everything . . ." Bradbury reports, "I'm a child of motion pictures." Prophetically, the first film Bradbury was taken to see, at the age of three, was the horror classic "The Hunchback of Notre Dame" starring Lon Chaney. Bradbury's teenage Aunt Neva whetted the boy's appetite for fantasy by reading the Oz books to him when he was six. As a child, Bradbury was also encouraged to read the classic Norse, Roman and Greek myths. When he grew old enough to choose his own reading material, the boy rapidly developed a fondness for the stories of Edgar Rice Burroughs and the comic book heroes Flash Gordon, Buck Rogers, and Prince Valiant. It was during his years in Waukegan, too, that Bradbury developed his interest in drama and acting, and, after witnessing a performance by the magician Blackstone, a lifelong passion for magic.

In 1932, his family moved to Tucson, Arizona. The talents Bradbury had developed as an amateur magician in Waukegan landed him a job at the local radio station. "I was on the radio every Saturday night reading comic strips to the kiddies and being paid in free tickets, to the local cinema, where I saw 'The Mummy,' 'The Murders in the Wax Museum,' 'Dracula' . . . and 'King Kong.' " The family stayed in Tucson for only a year, but Bradbury recalls "It was one of the greatest years of my life because I was acting and singing in operettas and writing, beginning to write my first short stories."

In 1934 the family moved to Los Angeles, where Bradbury has lived ever since. He attended Los Angeles High School, where he wrote and took part in a number of dramatic productions. His literary tastes were broadened to include Thomas Wolfe and Ernest Hemingway when he took a creative writing course. In the 1938 Los Angeles High School yearbook, the following prediction appeared with Bradbury's picture:

> Likes to write stories
> Admired as a thespian
> Headed for literary distinction

After graduation from high school Bradbury sold newspapers until he saved enough money to buy a typewriter and rent a small office. By the early '40s his stories appeared regularly in *Weird Tales.* "I sold a story every month there for three or four years when I was (in my early twenties). Made the magnificent sum of $20 for each story." Bradbury sold his first stories in 1945 to "slick" magazines—*Collier's, Charm,* and *Mademoiselle.*

Shortly after his marriage to Marguerite Susan McClure in 1947, Bradbury's first book, *Dark Carnival,* was published by Arkham House. About this time, the idea for an important book about Mars, a collection of loosely connected stories something like Sherwood Anderson's *Winesburg, Ohio* began to take definite shape, and in 1950, *The Martian Chronicles* was published. This marked the turning point in Bradbury's career. Though his appreciation by a wider audience did not come suddenly, it did proceed steadily, encouraged by the release of *The Illustrated Man* and the appearance of "The Beast from 20,000 Fathoms" in *The Saturday Evening Post* in 1951. In recent years, Bradbury's fictional output has dwindled, but he is in considerable demand as a lecturer, and his literary output has expanded to include screenplays, poetry, essays, reviews, and even grand opera.

Since the chronological order of Bradbury's stories and books is given little consideration in the rest of the book, it may be helpful to pay brief attention to it here. As already noted, Bradbury began regularly publishing short stories in the pulp magazines during the 1940s, and twenty-seven of these were collected in the book *Dark Carnival*. The edition was a limited one and has been out of print for some years. Following the publication of *The Martian Chronicles*, and as Bradbury's audience began to widen, he began to place stories in an increasing number of "slick" magazines, such as *Collier's*, *The Saturday Evening Post*, *Maclean's* (Canada), and *Esquire*. By the early '60s, Bradbury was being published almost exclusively by the major magazines, including *Harper's*, *McCall's*, *Life*, and *Playboy*.

The first major collection of short stories to be published after *Dark Carnival* was *The Illustrated Man* (1951). Thereafter followed *The Golden Apples of the Sun* (1953); *The October Country* (1955); *A Medicine for Melancholy* (1959); *The Machineries of Joy* (1964); *I Sing the Body Electric!* (1969); and *Long After Midnight* (1976). After *The Martian Chronicles*, the following novels were published: *Fahrenheit 451* (1953); *Dandelion Wine* (1957); *Something Wicked This Way Comes* (1962). These books represent the basic body of Bradbury's fiction. It is a testimony to Bradbury's popularity that, in spite of the fact that short story collections do not tend to sell well, all of the above books—with the exception of *Dark Carnival*—are still in print.

From time to time, other collections of short stories have been issued, but these have been mostly recombinations of tales from the collections above, with perhaps a few previously uncollected stories added. These include: *R Is For Rocket* (1962); *The Vintage Ray Bradbury* (1965—Bradbury's own selection of his best stories); *S Is for Space* (1966); and *Twice 22* (1966—*The Golden Apples of the Sun* and *A Medicine for Melancholy* combined).

Though he has been encouraged and assisted by a number of friends and teachers whom he recalls with great fondness, Ray Bradbury is largely a self-taught writer. In his introduction to the 1976 printing of the paperback *Dandelion Wine* he writes, "In my early twenties I floundered into a word-association process in which I simply got out of bed each morning, walked to my desk, and put down any word or series of words that happened along in my head. I would then take arms against the word, or for it, and bring on an assortment of characters to weigh the word and show me its meaning in my own life. An hour or two hours later, to my amazement, a new story would be finished and done."

Having come up with the method, Bradbury settled into a regimen very much like the one he recommends to would-be writers: "Something like this. 1,000 or 2,000 words every day for the next twenty years. . . . You might as well start now and get the necessary work done."

As for motivation, Bradbury feels that the needs of the commercial marketplace should not be a writer's prime consideration: "The answer to writing is always loving. If you don't love a thing you shouldn't be doing it. . . . I (don't) make intellectual decisions, because they're always wrong. If you think, if you plan a thing, then you're a market person. Then you make mistakes."

Bradbury credits his intuition with leading him to try an innovative way of selling his stories: "When I was 25, 26, I began to experiment with sending my short stories to places where they couldn't be accepted." Convinced that most editors were bored with seeing the same sort of material arriving day after day, Bradbury resolved to submit stories which, at least on the face of it, seemed inappropriate to the publication involved. Rather than send "Dandelion Wine" (later a chapter in the novel) to *Collier's* or *Mademoiselle,* therefore, Bradbury sent it to *Gourmet,* which didn't publish fiction. It was immediately accepted. "The Kilimanjaro Device" was snapped up by *Life,* which also didn't publish fiction, after the story had been rejected by most of the big fiction magazines. In these matters and in many others involving the things he enjoys and the tasks he undertakes, Bradbury insists that he places complete faith in his loves and intuitions to see him through.

In the world of fiction, and fantastic fiction in particular, Ray Bradbury stands as a somewhat awkward colossus, with one foot amid the tree-lined streets of Green Town, Illinois in the 1920s and '30s, and the other foot planted on the red sands of Mars in the not-too-distant future. Uncomfortable as this position may seem, it represents not only the basic thrust of Bradbury's work—from past to future, youth to manhood, Earth to the planets and stars—but also the actual trend of history for members of Bradbury's generation. Green Town and Mars represent the poles of Bradbury's fictional universe, the former embodying his own home town of Waukegan, the latter expressing his dreams and hopes about humanity's future. Green Town of the 1920s and Mars of the 21st century also represent a continuum of time along which most of his other stories are strung.

Bradbury's stories may look to the past with nostalgia, toward the future with awe, or may contemplate the present with terror or laughter, but in all cases they develop an imaginative intensity which provides the reader with a vivid experience in the here-and-now.

It is the experiential aspect of Bradbury's stories, the feeling that something has *happened* to the reader, that is perhaps their outstanding feature. The effect is achieved through the generation of strong sensory images, sensations of sight, touch, or sound, which one tends to recall long after the characters or plot have been forgotten. The term "poetic" is often applied to Bradbury's prose, and this certainly is suggested by the lyrical, frequently musical quality of many passages. A number of traditional poetic devices are also to be found, such as repeated stress patterns, alliteration, and internal rhymes. As to the origin of his favorite literary device, Bradbury recalls that his reading of Greek, Norse, and Roman mythology trained him at a very early age in the art of making metaphors. He sees this as part of his writing's continuing appeal: "Any of us who wish to exist beyond our time have to speak in tongues, have to speak in metaphors."

When describing an object or situation, Bradbury will often use a different metaphor or simile for each part, as if moving a spotlight over the thing, building it up in our minds out of a number of separate pictures. Each picture will have a different emotional tint according to the metaphor used, so that the completed image has an emotional as well as visual richness. For example, consider this description of *Tyrannosaurus rex* as the beast suddenly makes its appearance:

> A sound of thunder . . .
> It came on great oiled, resilient, striding legs. It towered thirty feet above half of the trees, a great evil god, folding its delicate watchmaker's claws close to its oily reptilian chest. Each lower leg was a piston, a thousand pounds of white bone, sunk in thick ropes of muscle, sheathed over in a gleam of pebbled skin like the mail of a terrible warrior. Each thigh was a ton of meat, ivory, and steel mesh. And from the great breathing cage of the upper body those two delicate arms dangled out front, arms with hands which might pick up and examine men like toys, while the snake neck coiled.

The creature is assembled like a jigsaw puzzle out of strikingly juxtaposed images—god, watchmaker, warrior, snake. At the same time, depictions of movement—striding, towering, folding, breathing, dangling—keep the creature alive every step of the way. Most of the metaphors in this passage have common associations; we expect most readers to build up pretty much the same picture of the monster, because most people would probably agree on what a watchmaker's claws, pistons, ropes of muscle, chain mail, and a snake neck would look like. But in some of his more intriguing passages, Bradbury will use similes or metaphors that have no commonly agreed-upon associations, but that suggest sometimes subtle, sometimes markedly different pictures to different readers. Reading such a passage becomes an experience, then, which seems very personal. Here, for instance, is a passage in which the mythical inventor of the fog horn tells how he conceived of his device:

> I'll make a voice like all of time and all of the fog that ever was; I'll make a voice that is like an empty bed beside you all night long, and like an empty house when you open the door, and like trees in autumn with no leaves. A sound like birds flying south, crying, and a sound like November wind and the sea on the hard, cold shore. . . . They'll call it a Fog Horn and whoever hears it will know the sadness of eternity and the briefness of life.

Some of these similes touch upon familiar sounds—the crying of birds, the crashing of the sea. Some are free for considerable interpretation—what is the sound of an empty house when you open the door? But others force the reader to participate in creating the image in a way unique to each person. Each reader must imagine for himself what a voice like "all of time," "all the fog that ever was," or "an empty bed beside you all night long" would sound like. The reader must recall the feeling of loneliness, which of course these images are intended to suggest, from his own particular experience. This cooperation in the imaginative act which Bradbury elicits in such cases accounts for much of the pleasure his stories provide.

As may be gathered from the examples above, Bradbury is
something of an impressionistic writer, building up his scenes
indirectly with a barrage of images, using suggestion and implication rather than direct exposure. When required, his sentence structure may be quite flexible, the overriding purpose
of a passage taking precedence over elegance of grammar. In
"The One Who Waits," a being who has taken over the mind of
a man describes the feeling as the man tries to regain control:

> (I hear) a voice calling deep within me, tiny and
> afraid. And the voice cries, *Let me go, let me go,* and there
> is a feeling as if something is trying to get free, a pound-
> ing of labyrinthine doors, a rushing down dark cor-
> ridors and up passages, echoing and screaming.

As the syntax of the second sentence becomes increasingly
shaky, the meaning becomes increasingly clear.

Of course, Bradbury's enthusiasm sometimes goes a bit too
far, and most readers will encounter stories in which they feel
oversaturated with imagery, lost in a sea of Irish dialect, or
perhaps turned off by a robot version of George Bernard Shaw
that is a little too wise for its own good.

Bradbury's lifelong interest in drama has helped him to
develop a sharp ear for speech patterns, and he is particularly
good at developing a sense of uneasiness or menace through
dialogue. In "Dark They Were, and Golden-Eyed," Harry
Bittering begins to notice subtle changes in his fellow earthmen, leading him to suspect that Mars, which they have inher-
ited from the extinct, golden-eyed Martians, is beginning to
exert an unwholesome influence:

> "Sam," Bittering said, "Your eyes—"
> "What about them, Harry?"
> "Didn't they used to be grey?"
> "Well now, I don't remember."
> "They were, weren't they?"
> "Why do you ask, Harry?"

"Because now they're kind of yellow-colored."
"Is that so, Harry?" Sam said, casually.

Another example which comes to mind is the entire story "A Flight of Ravens," with its bitter exchanges between the successful writer and the unhappy friends he is visiting. As has been mentioned earlier, Bradbury regards himself as an entertainer, and his stories are intended primarily to amuse. But this is not to say that the tales do not contain, or may not be appreciated on, deeper levels. From his youngest days as a writer, Bradbury seems to have been aware that the simple entertainments of American popular culture, such as horror movies, comic books, or carnival rides expressed, in powerful if primitive metaphors, many of the deeper fears and fantasies of their audiences. In horror movies, for instance, fears of the dark might be symbolized by a leering vampire, the impulse to destruction might be embodied in a rampaging gorilla. In a carnival ride, such as a roller coaster, the rider may experience, in a safe context, the visceral fear of impending death many times over, his laughter at the ride's conclusion reaffirming life after all. In Bradbury's stories too, one surrenders to the dominant, if primitive, mood, and comes away from the last sentence with a heightened sensitivity to life. It is significant that carnival images appear regularly in Bradbury's fiction—most obviously in *Something Wicked This Way Comes,* but also in such characters as The Illustrated Man, the monsters, the magicians, and the machine-makers. The difference between Bradbury and, say, the designer of a roller coaster is that Bradbury is conscious of the link between his art, his own dreams, and the dreams of his audience. It is through maintaining a touchstone with the world of his own dreams, and with the world of dreams common to all of us, that Bradbury is able to charge his stories with their particular power.

Many of Bradbury's stories may also be viewed as metaphors for his own work as an artist. In "The Rocket," for example, Fiorello Bodoni builds a device which will take his children on an artificial, but enthralling trip through space. To a certain extent, of course, Bodoni is Bradbury himself. But it is important to realize that the children are Bradbury too. Bradbury the man writes to delight, amaze, or terrify the child in himself, and many stories reflect this very act. A significant number of stories are told from the viewpoint of children, who not only represent the emotional intensity of his own youth, but also represent the ideal audience for his magic—attentive, cooperative, and unquestioning. Time and again, Bradbury the adult—in the person of his characters Fiorello Bodoni, carnival-master Dark, or Colonel Freeleigh—entertains, frightens, or delights Bradbury the child—Paolo Bodoni, Will Halloway, Doug Spaulding.

Before proceeding to survey Bradbury's themes in specific stories, we will mention here some elements which appear so frequently in his fiction that it would become tedious to mention them every time they appear, but which the reader should be aware of in a general way. Two themes that appear constantly are reality as determined by point of view, and metamorphosis. In the world of Bradbury's fiction, reality is a very relative quantity. What an object is depends upon what a given character needs or wants it to be. We all, Bradbury seems to say, perceive our world through the strawberry window of our fantasies. "The Wonderful Ice Cream Suit" demonstrates how the same object—in this case a suit of clothes—can be "real" but in a different way to different people. "The Dwarf" uses the altered point of view provided by a fun house mirror to alter his perception of himself. And in "Night Meeting," from *The Martian Chronicles,* Gomez and the Martian both argue for the validity of their point of view across an unbridgeable gap in time. Because each person has his own fantasies, each person's view of reality is unique. We are all the center of our own worlds, and one of the subtler implications of Bradbury's fiction is that the journey of understanding between two individuals may be as challenging and rewarding as the journey from Earth to Mars.

Metamorphosis appears both by itself and mixed with the reality-as-point-of-view theme. Just as Zeus changed into a swan to obtain the favors of Leda, and Daphne was changed into a laurel tree to escape the attentions of Apollo, Bradbury's characters often are changed in response to their own or someone else's pressing need. The owners of the Wonderful Ice Cream Suit are changed into the romantic, self-confident, handsome men they wish themselves to be. The Strawberry Window changes the forbidding landscape of Mars into one reminiscent of home. The dwarf's fun house mirror changes him, at least temporarily, into someone tall and imposing. Again, objective reality is a solid, unchanging quantity, while fantasy is dynamic, constantly changing. Bradbury's theme of metamorphosis reaches its extreme on Mars, where men become Martians and Martians become men, where, in effect, we and our dreams change places with each other. But the theme, one of the most tangible results of Bradbury's reading of the classics, appears frequently throughout his work.

Another common element in Bradbury's work, less a theme perhaps than an aspect of his character, is a certain contrariness. Bradbury likes to play with ideas. He takes pleasure in challenging ideas enjoying general popularity, and takes just as much pleasure in challenging his own. To intellectual critics condemning comic books and other forms of popular literature, Bradbury responds with "Pillar of Fire." To Utopian visionaries extolling the virtues of a world run by machines, he counters with *Fahrenheit 451* or "The Pedestrain." On the other hand, as if to challenge his own grim picture of mechanized society, Bradbury has written such glowing paeans to robots as "G. B. S.—Mark V" and "I Sing the Body Electric." On a broader level, this contrariness extends into what might be viewed as Bradbury's philosophical position, a simple and steadfast optimism in the face of the world's naysayers and pessimists. This philosophy may be as narrowly expressed as Charles Halloway's challenge to the forces of death in *Something Wicked This Way Comes*—a challenge not too different from Alice's ". . . you're nothing but a pack of cards!" Or it may be expressed on a cosmic scale as in Bradbury's original cantata *Christus Apollo,* in which man is enjoined to negate the threat of death by saying yes to the challenge of the stars.

2

medicines for melancholy

Magic · Horror · Death

■ Magic is a pervasive theme in Bradbury's work. This might have been foreordained the day in 1931 when, during a performance in Waukegan, the great magician Blackstone presented eleven-year-old Bradbury with a live rabbit. In any case, that incident reflects the type of magic usually found in Bradbury's work, that is: theatrical magic, legerdemain, as opposed to anything genuinely supernatural. For Bradbury, the magical power certain people and things seem to have lies in their capacity to stimulate, expand, or sustain the imagination. They accomplish this by altering our perception and challenging our view of reality, so that we are led to view things in a fresh, new way. This process is more interesting, Bradbury seems to say, than anything truly miraculous. Should a sorcerer literally create a rabbit out of thin air, little would be accomplished outside of our being intimidated by his power. But when the theatrical magician pulls his rabbit out of a hat, we know it is a trick, and because we know it is a trick we are amused, intrigued, and our curiosity is aroused.

Bradbury is, of course, a self-styled story-telling magician, and though within a particular story his brand of magic may be thwarted, misused, or may backfire, still the story itself will like as not lead us to, and sharpen our awareness of, that point where reality and imagination meet, where imagination may restructure reality and create a new order.

Magic People

Lacking supernatural powers, Bradbury's magicians use inborn talents and acquired skills to perform their wonders. The old man in "To the Chicago Abyss" is blessed—or in his case, perhaps, cursed—with a vivid memory and an eloquent tongue. He wanders about in a world devastated by atomic war, recalling for whoever will listen what it was like before the holocaust. The man cannot stop himself, even though he is constantly being hunted by the special police who regard him as a source of unrest. The old man's magic is his ability to recall the details of the past so vividly that his listeners are transported there. For some, the experience is too painful, and hence, terrifying, as when the old man takes a woman by surprise:

> "Coffee."
> The woman gasped and stiffened.
> The old man's gnarled fingers tumbled in pantomine on his unseen lap.
> "Twist the key! Bright-red, yellow-letter can! Compressed air. Hisss! Vacuum pack, Ssst! Like a snake! . . . The scent, the odor, the smell. Rich, dark, wondrous Brazilian beans, fresh-ground!"
> Leaping up, reeling as if gun-shot, the woman tottered.

Though his behavior is a bit bizarre, the man is still a professional. He recognizes his talent and employs it in what he regards as a socially useful way:

What did I have to offer a world that was forgetting? My memory! . . . I found the more I remembered, the more I *could* remember! Depending on who I sat down with, I remembered imitation flowers, dial telephones, refrigerators, kazoos (you ever play a kazoo?), thimbles, bicycle clips, not bicycles, no, bicycle *clips*! isn't that wild and strange?

This old man is the quintessential Bradbury magician. He embodies characteristics of people and objects found throughout Bradbury's work in this ability to conjure up the past, to evoke nostalgia through the *experience* of another time.

If the old man's talent is a bit dangerous in view of the society in which he finds himself, a similar talent is fatal to Leonard Mark in "The Visitor." Leonard arrives on Mars and is greeted by a number of homesick exiles from Earth. One of them, Saul, asks Leonard what New York is like now.

"Like this," said Leonard Mark. And he looked at Saul.
New York grew up out of the desert, made of stone and filled with March winds. Neons exploded in electric color. Yellow taxis glided in a still night. Bridges rose and tugs chanted in the midnight harbor. Curtains rose on spangled musicals.
Saul put his hands to his head, violently.
"Hold on, hold on!" he cried. "what's happening to me?"

Though Mark is telepathic, and able to impress his vision directly upon another's mind, his effect is similar to that produced by the old man. But where the old man's talent was appreciated by only a few of his fellows, Mark's ability puts him very much in demand. In a short time, greed and exploitation take their toll—the exiles begin to fight over exclusive rights to Mark, and in the struggle, he is killed.

There is a modest echo of this exploitation of another person's talent in "The Great Wide World Over There." The story explores the relativity of power by showing how a perfectly modest talent may seem great, even magical, to someone with no power at all. Cora and Tom live in isolation in the mountains and are illiterate. When they are visited by their nephew Benjy, who can read and write, it is as though a guest from another world has arrived.

A simple object like Benjy's pencil is almost a magic wand to Cora's eyes: "She wanted to touch the pencil, but hadn't touched one in years because it made her feel foolish and then angry and then sad." Benjy writes letters all over the world for Cora, mostly to companies, asking for free booklets. Though she cannot read any of these, Cora feels in touch with the world beyond the horizon as the junk mail pours in. But she is dependent on Benjy to sustain this miracle, and the door to it closes forever when Benjy leaves.

"The Man in the Rorschach Shirt" is a more active magician. Once a world-renowned psychiatrist, Immanuel Brokaw has taken his practice underground. Wearing a shirt with crazy patterns on it, he strolls about the beaches of California, and when he meets someone who is troubled, he attempts to cure them in his own unusual way.

> I walk along in my own time and way and come on people and let the wind flap my great sailcloth shirt now veering north, south, or south-by-west and watch their eyes pop, glide, leer, squint, wonder. And when a certain person says a certain word about my ink-slashed cotton colors I give pause. I chat. I walk with them awhile. We peer into the great glass of the sea. I sidewise peer into their soul. Sometimes we stroll for hours, a longish session with the weather. Usually it takes but that one day and, not knowing with whom they walked, scot-free, they are discharged all unwitting patients.

Bradbury suggests that the storyteller, the psychic, the literate relative, the psychiatrist can all seem like magicians, given the right contexts. They alter our reality and we don't know how they do it. The musician can also have this power, and Bradbury explores this idea twice in "Getting Through

Sunday Somehow" and "The Day It Rained Forever." Interestingly enough, both musicians are women, and both are harpists. The first story concerns a man wandering the streets of Dublin in a depressed mood. Suddenly he hears a tune being played by an old woman with a harp, and "as if a cork had been pulled, all the heavy gray sea waters vanished down a hole in my shoe; I felt my sadness go." When the man tries to tell the old woman of the effect she has had on him, he sounds as if he is recovering from a magic spell:

> Imagine you're an American writer, looking for material, far from home, wife, children, friends, in a hard winter, in a cheerless hotel, on a bad gray day with naught but broken glass, chewed tobacco, and sooty snow in your soul. Imagine you're walking in the damned winter streets and turn a corner, and there's this little woman with a golden harp and everything she plays is another season, autumn, spring, summer, coming, going in a free-for-all. And the ice melts, the fog lifts, the wind burns with June, and ten years shuck off your life.

A different change of climate is called for in "The Day It Rained Forever," which takes place in a seedy hotel that "stood like a hollowed dry bone under the very center of the desert sky where the sun burned the roof all day." What the sweltering clients need is a miracle, and a miracle worker arrives in the form of Miss Hillgood. Like the old lady in Dublin, Miss Hillgood uses her music to produce a much-appreciated change of climate:

> Each time her fingers moved, the rain fell pattering through the dark hotel. The rain fell cool at the open windows and the rain rinsed down the baked floor boards of the porch. . . . But more than anything the soft touch and coolness of it fell on Mr. Smith and Mr. Terle. . . . Seated there, they felt their heads tilt slowly back to let the rain fall where it would.

So it is that Bradbury's artist-magicians operate on three levels: changing the apparent climate, the emotional state of their audience, and ultimately the feelings of the reader.

"The Drummer Boy of Shiloh," also a musician of sorts, is not aware of the power his skill holds until his General tells him that his drumming is the heartbeat of the army. The tempo the drummer sets during battle may spell the difference between victory and defeat, because, the General says, "blood moving fast in them does indeed make men feel as they'd put on steel."

Bradbury sees the technician too as a kind of magician, insofar as he changes the way in which reality is viewed. In "Tyrannosaurus Rex" we meet a Hollywood special effects expert. John Terwilliger is a specialist in three-dimensional animation. He is apparently patterned after Willis O'Brien, creator of King Kong, or Ray Harryhausen, Bradbury's friend and creator of the monster in "The Beast from 20,000 Fathoms." Terwilliger performs his magic in his studio, photographing miniature jungles and foot-high dinosaurs so that they appear to be full size on the movie screen. "Rubber, steel, clay, reptilian latex sheath, glass eye, porcelain fang, all ambles, trundles, strides in terrible prides through continents as yet unmanned, by seas as yet unsalted, a billion years lost away. They *do* breathe. They *do* smite the air with thunders. Oh, uncanny!"

Bradbury's magician does not always seek to affect the world at large. Sometimes his skills may be used to promote his own domestic tranquillity, as in the case of Fiorello Bodoni. Bodoni, a poor junk dealer, cannot afford to send his family on an actual rocket trip, so he buys a scrap, mock-up rocket and rigs it electronically for a facsimile trip around Mars. Bodoni's wife knows, but the children do not, that "The Rocket" is not real, still the joyful artifice of it appeals to her: "Perhaps . . . perhaps, some night, you might take me on just a little trip, do you think?"

In "The Best of All Possible Worlds" it is the husband who profits from his wife's skills. Mr. "Smith's" wife is an accomplished actress, who keeps her husband from seeking other women by frequently altering her appearance and becoming any sort of woman he might desire. Both Mr. Smith and Mrs. Bodoni enjoy their partners' artifices, and become for them an audience—something that is essential to the magician and the fiction writer as well. An audience prepared to employ what Coleridge calls "that willing suspension of disbelief for the moment, which constitutes poetic faith." Viewed this way, magic can be regarded as a kind of conspiracy wherein artist and audience agree to experience the joy of magic by playing their respective parts. This can backfire occasionally, as Bradbury suggests in "Invisible Boy." Old Lady, living a lonely life in the Ozark Mountains, tries to trick her visiting relative Charlie into prolonging his stay with her by promising to teach him how to make himself invisible. The trick is accomplished simply by Old Lady pretending she can't see Charlie any more. This soon becomes quite a strain as Charlie takes advantage of his invisibility to dash about stark naked. Old Lady must then trick Charlie into becoming "visible" again.

The theme of a boy trying to exercise his personal magic power takes on poignant overtones in "The Miracles of Jamie." Here we find magician and audience combined in one person as Jamie tries to convince himself that he has magical power and that through it he can make his dying mother well. But, though it is not always clear, there is a dividing line between a "willing suspension of disbelief" and simple self-deception. Jamie crosses that line with tragic consequences.

> Inside the walls of Jericho that was Jamie's mind, a thought went screaming about in one last drive of power: Yes, she's dead, all right, so she is dead, so what if she is dead? Bring her back to life again, yes, make her live again, Lazarus, come forth, Lazarus, Lazarus, come forth from the tomb, Lazarus come forth.
>
> He must have been babbling aloud, for Dad turned and glared at him in old, ancient horror and struck him bluntly across the mouth to shut him up.
>
> Jamie sank against the bed, mouthing into the cold blankets, and the walls of Jericho crumbled and fell down about him.

Magic Things

Human beings are not the only sources of magic for Bradbury. Animals and physical objects may also affect our reality in mysterious ways. Certainly Martin's dog in "The Emissary" has a certain magical effect, aside from the dreadful supernatural powers it seems to exercise at the end of the story. The dog does not change reality for Martin, but rather deepens and broadens it. The boy cannot venture into the world outside his bedroom but the dog can, and brings back touches of it that enrich the invalid's life.

The bird in "The Parrot Who Met Papa" is another magical animal with a fabulous memory that the characters in the story suspect might include Hemingway's last, unwritten novel. Another magic fowl is the namesake of "The Inspired Chicken Motel," a bird whose eggs seem to have the gift of prophesy.

Inanimate things can be magical too. This is not a surprising suggestion from a writer such as Bradbury, for whom nostalgia is so important. The ability of an object to recall the past from which it came, and so to generate a whole complex of emotional responses, can certainly transcend whatever practical function the object might have had. Other objects may possess qualities that allow them to transform the present, and in so doing, alter the shape of the future. Of course, such power often does not lie within the object itself, but rather within the mind of the beholder. In this case, the magical effect an object has may depend upon the state of the mind perceiving it.

We find an unhealthy mind in "And So Died Riabouchinska," a classic story of a schizophrenic ventriloquist who loses control over what his dummy says. Fabian's dummy, Riabouchinska, was modeled after a woman Fabian once loved. Since the dummy represents the better half of Fabian's mind, Fabian can no longer control it after he has committed murder.

Many minds contemplate the contents of "The Jar" which Charlie buys at a carnival and brings home to show off to his neighbors. Everyone is curious about what the jar holds, and

Gramps finds himself lying awake nights to "think about that jar settin' here in the long dark. Think about it hangin' in liquid, peaceful and pale like an animal oyster. Sometimes I wake Maw and we both think on it ..." Juke, recalling how he once drowned a kitten, sees his own guilt in the jar: "I know to this day the way that kitten floated after it was all over, driftin' aroun', slow and not worryin', lookin' out at me, not condemnin' me for what I done. But not likin' me, neither. Ahhhh. . . ." Jahdoo has a more mystical explanation: "That be the center of Life, sure 'nuff!. . . That am Middibamboo Mama, from which we all come ten thousand years ago. Believe it!" And Mrs. Tridden, whose child was lost in the swamp years ago, sees through eyes burdened with loss: "My baby . . . my baby. My Foley, Foley! Foley, is that you?"

In "The Jar," Bradbury suggests that magic can be a function of need. Given an ambiguous situation or object, an imaginative viewer may fantasize a new reality based on his personal need to enrich, repair, complete or transcend his life. This theme is explored again in "A Miracle of Rare Device." Two drifters travelling through the Arizona desert stumble across a spot on the roadside from which an unusual mirage may be seen. As the two men watch, a wonderful city seems to rise up against the distant mountains. The two men set up a sign and charge twenty-five cents for passing motorists to stop and see the view. Soon they discover that everyone who stops sees a different city in the mirage. One man sees Paris, another Rome, still another sees fabled Xanadu with its "sunny pleasure-dome with caves of ice!" The spot is magic because it nurtures imagination. It is interesting that the villain of the piece, Ned Hopper, sees no mirage at all. And when Hopper files a claim on the roadside spot, evicts his rivals, and takes over their business, the magic in the spot vanishes. None of the people who stop when Hopper is present see anything at all. The drifter Robert understands: "Right now I'm feeling sorry for Ned Hopper. . . . He never saw what we saw. He never saw what anybody saw. He never believed for one second. And you know what? Disbelief is catching. It rubs off on people."

As important to Bradbury as magic which manifests itself in a public way, is magic which operates on a more intimate level affecting one or more individuals. It is not surprising, given Bradbury's passion for nostalgia, that most of these items of intimate magic are connected in some way with the past. There is the wonderful brass bed in "The Marriage Mender." The bed has been in Antonio's family since "before Garibaldi!" It is one of the few valuable possessions belonging to the Italian immigrant and his wife, Maria. But so far it has failed to cooperate with Antonio and Maria's attempts to conceive a child. Fortunately, the bed is imbued with enough trappings of Bradbury magic—a "shimmering harp," a "fabulous dream machine"—to fulfill its function before Antonio is foolish enough to replace it.

Then there is "The Pumpernickel," a common loaf of bread that sets Mr. Welles off on a lengthy reminiscence about his old gang. Mr. Welles eventually learns to let the past go, but this is not so easy for some lonely settlers on Mars in "The Strawberry Window."

Bob and Carrie live in a tin shack in a frontier town on Mars. Both are terribly homesick. Carrie wants to return home, but Bob wants to stick it out anyway. In a desperate move, Bob spends all of the family's savings on artifacts from their old home on earth—a piano, a bed, some parlor furniture, and the entire front porch. Most important in terms of its magical effect, and its symbolic relation to all the other objects, is the front door with its stained glass window. The window alters the color of things viewed beyond it. It changes perception in a comforting way because of the associations it conjures up. When viewed through the panels of colored glass, the alien planet seems more like home:

> There was Mars, with its cold sky warmed and its dead seas fired with color, with its hills like mounds of strawberry ice, and its sand like burning charcoals sifted by the wind. The strawberry window, the strawberry window, breathed soft rose colors on the land and filled the mind and the eye with the light of a never-ending dawn.

This putting on, in effect, of rose-colored glasses is not the escape from reality the gesture ordinarily implies. For Bradbury, this deliberate alteration of perception forms a bridge between old reality and new. In looking through the glass, Bob and Carrie are reminded of the underlying similarities between their old home and their new one, and hence of the continuity of their lives. This artifact from the past gives them the strength to face the future. Bradbury seems most happy with illusions of this sort, which bring about recognition rather than mystification.

Of course, an object suffused with the magic of nostalgia can be a springboard to escape, and Bradbury treats this idea handsomely in "A Scent of Sarsaparilla." The object in question is a whole room, appropriately an attic. Mr. Finch retires to his attic to escape the cold of winter and his nagging wife, Cora. The attic is the ideal room for Bradbury, jammed as it is with nostalgia-laden objects from the past. If a single one such as the strawberry window can have a wonderful effect, then the potential of a whole roomful of such objects can be awesome. In this case, the cumulative power of the furnishings of Mr. Finch's attic is so great that it accomplishes a real feat of magic and literally transports Finch back in time. It may seem to be cheating a bit, in the context of these other stories, for Bradbury to introduce genuine magic in this way. But the story profits from the irony of the attic being a real time machine, and in any case, Finch's surrender to the emotional spell of the attic is complete even before he steps out of the window into the past.

Perhaps Bradbury's most famous and beautifully drawn magical device is "The Wonderful Ice Cream Suit." In this tale, science fiction and fantastic elements are combined in an essentially straight story, replete with humor and sharp characterization. The centerpiece of the story is, of course, the suit itself. For the six Mexican Americans who individually lack sufficient money to buy it, the white suit represents a technology almost beyond their comprehension. Each is convinced that if he could possess the suit his entire life would be changed

for the better. The connection with science fiction is subtle, yet
here is a manufactured object which can change the shape of
the future. But the suit is possessed of magical qualities, too,
for it can fulfill wishes. The only problem is: how to possess it?
It is Gomez who hits upon the idea of rounding up six men of
about the same size, each with ten dollars in his pocket: "Are we
not fine? . . . All the same size, all the same dream—the suit. So
each of us will look beautiful at least one night each week, eh?"

The suit is a vehicle too for Bradbury's pet themes of
metamorphosis and point-of-view altering reality. The suit
changes each man who wears it, allowing him to fulfill his
personal dreams of power, sexual attractiveness, or economic
well being. At the same time, each man acknowledges the
appeal the suit has for the others, and in so doing, invests the
suit with a kind of objective power. It may be said that the suit
wears the man just as much as the man wears the suit. The ice
cream suit is probably Bradbury's most well-rounded magical
device. It is more than just the vehicle for an individual's
escape into fantasy or nostalgia. It forms a bond of understanding and affection among the men, allowing them, however
briefly, to transcend their individual poverty and loneliness.
At the same time, the men realize that their humble circumstances are just the setting the suit requires to perform its
magic. As Martinez notes, "If we ever get rich . . . it'll be kind of
sad. Then we'll all have suits. And there won't be no more
nights like tonight. It'll break up the old gang. It'll never be the
same after that."

Horror

The horror story is not just a story in which something frightening happens. In the tradition of such masters as Poe and
Lovecraft before him, Bradbury's horror stories touch upon
some of the deepest human fears and superstitions.

The emotional and visceral effect that a well written horror
story has on the reader is usually produced by a rigorous,

almost mathematical structure. There is an underlying formula that the reader follows, at least subconsciously. This may
be a simple face-the-consequence formula, in which the main
character makes a pact with the devil or performs a similar rash
act. Or a situation may be set up which, if repeated with certain
variations, could precipitate dire results. For example, a child
is characterized with the habit of opening a particular drawer
to locate a toy pistol hidden there. Should the toy pistol be
replaced with a real one, the child's innocent action creates a
situation fraught with terror. The underlying structure of a
good horror story educates the reader to the ground rules of
the tale, maintains a sense of unity through the emotional
turmoil, and provides a sense of inevitability at the ending. To
appreciate Bradbury's use of structure in his horror stories, we
will look at two of them in some detail.

"The Emissary" is a fine example of the effective use of
structure. Little Martin is an invalid whose main contact with
the outside world is through his Dog. The story consists
primarily of three visits which the dog makes to Martin's bedroom. The first visit establishes the pattern of all of the dog's
visits. We learn that Dog dashes out of doors to play for a while,
then bounds back indoors, upstairs, and into Martin's bed. By
inhaling the odor of the dog's coat and examining the fragments of leaf and twig clinging to it, Martin is able to recon-
struct the season, the weather, and the path that Dog has
followed: ". . . Dog had rattled down hills where autumn lay in
cereal crispness, where children lay in funeral pyres, in rustl-
ing heaps, the leaf-buried but watchful dead, as Dog and the
world blew by." In the opening pages of the story, we are also
introduced to the fact that Dog has a bad habit of digging holes
where he is not supposed to. Dog's second visit to the bedroom
reveals his function of bringing guests to Martin's bedside. On
this occasion, it is Martin's favorite visitor, Miss Haight, his
school teacher. After this second visit, Miss Haight is killed in
an automobile accident. Some weeks later, Dog runs off and
disappears. It is then contrived for Martin to be left alone in

the house late one night, thus setting the stage for Dog's third visit. Dog's third visit follows the pattern of those already established. Because of this, the reader is able to notice ominous little variations in the pattern which suggest that something may be amiss. The dog is heard barking a long way off, drawing nearer, then farther away again. Martin wonders at this, but we see the implication that the dog is guiding someone along the way—someone who cannot move as fast as he can. Finally Dog is right outside the house. The downstairs door opens—"Someone was kind enough to have opened the door for Dog." The dog dashes upstairs and jumps onto the bed as usual, and as usual, Martin begins his detective work to see where the dog has been. The sensory picture here is as vivid as ever, but this time quite disturbing:

> It was a smell of strange earth. It was a smell of night within night, the smell of digging down deep in shadow through earth that had lain cheek by jowl with things that were long hidden and decayed . . .
> What kind of message was this from Dog? What could such a message mean? The stench—the ripe and awful cemetery earth.

There are only nine sentences left in the story by this time, but no more are needed. We cannot escape the conclusion even if we stop reading. Bradbury does not even have to use much description, for our imaginations are already at work constructing the horror which Martin finally hears climbing the stairs "one foot dragged after the other, painfully, slowly . . ." Bradbury has the excellent good taste to end the story with the words—"Martin had company."—the same words which preceded Miss Haight's first visit to the room. "The Emissary" is a classic tribute to the sort of Halloween story told around campfires. Its emotional effect almost buries the meticulous precision of its structure. Looking back over the story, it is possible to find many subtle touches contributing to the pervasive sense of death at the conclusion. For instance, even in the passage quoted above regarding Dog's first visit, a passage intended to convey the crisp high spirits of an autumn afternoon, we find references to "funeral pyres," and "leaf-buried but watchful dead."

"The October Game" also uses a repeated event to involve the reader in the story, but in a different way. We are introduced at the outset to Mich Wilder's intention to do violence to his wife, but the means by which he is to achieve this is withheld for some time. Instead the story sets up the atmosphere of a Halloween party, and suggests that Wilder may try to get at his wife through their child. Suddenly we are in the darkened basement with the Wilders and some neighborhood children as the game called "the witch is dead" begins. As the supposed "parts" of a chopped-up witch are passed around the room, the explanation of what the parts actually are is suggested by the children: "He gets some old chicken innards from the icebox and hands them around and says, 'These are her innards!' And he makes a clay head and passes it for her head, and passes a soup bone for her arm . . ." Meanwhile Mrs. Wilder notices that her daughter is missing. Suddenly, the reader joins Mrs. Wilder in mentally replaying the game so far, this time with a macabre possibility very evident. Our discoveries accompany Mrs. Wilder's second by second, and the suspense, though sustained for only a short time, attains a high pitch. The ending is something of a throwaway, and the story is marred somewhat by its repellent theme, still the tale remains one of Bradbury's most memorable.

"The Emissary" and "The October Game" are organized to set the reader up for the shock of a surprise ending. In these cases it works because the surprise has been well organized. But stories with surprise endings are frequently unsatisfying since they leave the reader with a sense of having been tricked. Most exciting horror tales, Bradbury's included, are stories of suspense in which the lay of the plot is revealed very early, and the reader is kept on edge awaiting the outcome. Alfred Hitchcock has very effectively distinguished between surprise and suspense. Surprise, according to Hitchock, is when we watch two men having a conversation and suddenly a bomb located under their table goes off. There has been no preparation, so the effect is brief. If however, we know beforehand that the bomb is under the table, and we know what time it is going to go off, and we can see a clock on the wall behind the men, then the entire scene becomes charged with suspense. In this case, says Hitchcock, ". . . The public is participating in the scene. The audience is longing to warn the characters . . . 'You shouldn't be talking about such trivial matters. There's a bomb beneath you and it's about to explode!' "

Most of Bradbury's horror stories follow Hitchcock's principles of suspense and clue the reader in to what is going on quite early. The mother of "The Small Assassin" knows her baby is trying to kill her from the first line of the story. Young Charles in "Fever Dream" senses that his body is being taken over by some alien force on the first page. An invasion of Earth by creatures from another world is foreshadowed during the first few sentences of "Zero Hour" and "Boys! Raise Giant Mushrooms in *Your* Cellar!" Suspense leads to horror in these stories as the characters involved meet tragic fates.

Bradbury's horror stories, then, are primarily technical pieces aimed at achieving a narrow, specific effect. The stories demand a strict attention to form, and are not generally noted for subtlety of plot or characterization. An exception is "The Next in Line," a horror tale mixed with a skillful study of a deteriorating relationship. The story has all of the formal characteristics of the horror and suspense tale discussed so far. The crucial event of the tale, a visit to the cavern of the mummies of Guanajuato, is introduced on the first page, and the funeral of a child on the second page reaffirms the atmosphere of lurking death that builds toward the story's climax.

But the development of "The Next in Line" is much more extended and subtle than the average horror tale. The story examines in detail the shambles Marie and Joseph's marriage has become, primarily through Marie's eyes. The horrific element in the story, Marie's fear of dying and being hung among the mummies, does not represent an outside force intruding upon Marie's life, but a morbid development within her own mind. On the third page of the story, as she watches the child's funeral, Marie automatically refers to the child as female:

> She did not think it unusual, her choice of the feminine pronoun. Already she had identified herself with that tiny fragment parceled like an unripe variety of fruit. Now, in this moment, she was being carried up the hill within compressing darkness, a stone in a peach, silent and terrified, the touch of the father against the coffin material outside; gentle and noiseless and firm inside.

The rest of the story traces Marie's gradual surrender of life into an embrace of death. The mummies, horrible as they are, become merely symbolic of her obsession. In the end, we are not so much shocked by Marie's fate as by her husband's complicity in it.

Death

Bradbury does not like Marie's attitude of surrender. This is not surprising from a man who in recent years has vigorously espoused the conquest of space as the surest way of guaranteeing humankind's immortality. One senses Bradbury is more sympathetic with Aunt Tildy in "There Was an Old Woman," who, when Death calls upon her in the guise of a handsome gentleman, is quite rebellious: "You just skit out of here; don't bother me, I got my tattin' and knittin' to do, and no never minds about tall, dark gentlemen with fangled ideas." When Death succeeds in lulling Tildy to sleep long enough for him to separate her body from her soul, the irascible old lady's spirit counters by marching to the mortuary and reclaiming her body.

Bradbury was profoundly affected by his visit to Mexico, shortly after the end of World War II, during the festival of *El Dia de Muerte*—the day of death. There is more about this visit in Chapter 8, but the important thing to be noted here is the extent to which Bradbury was struck by Death as an over-whelming tangible reality. Stories such as "The Next in Line" and "*El Dia de Muerte*" directly reflect the vividness of this experience. Death as involved in these stories is crushingly final; once it has entered and taken effect, there is nowhere for either character or writer to go. "*El Dia de Muerte*" concerns itself with three deaths—that of a boy named Raimundo (Bradbury's first name in Spanish), that of a bull in the ring, and that of another boy playing Christ on the cross at the top of a church steeple. The deaths are set against the celebrations throughout Mexico on the Day of the Dead. As part of the celebrations, candy skulls with different names on them are sold everywhere. Raimundo has one with his name on it which is shattered when he is hit by a car. At the story's conclusion, ". . . The sugar skull with the letters R and A and I and M and U and N and D and O was snatched up and eaten by children who fought over the name."

As if to liberate himself from the crushing finality of Death as an emotional force and as a subject in writing, Bradbury has occasionally taken a cue from the Mexicans and their candy skulls. He often, in effect, reduces Death to a palatable symbol, a somewhat theatrical figure in a Halloween costume whose mask, if somewhat frightening, is still only a mask. This is the case in "There Was an Old Woman," where Death, as a hand-some young man, is seen as no match for her vitality. It is the case again in "Death and the Maiden," in which another old lady, Old Mam, attempts to elude death by barricading herself inside the house. Death tries out various disguises, but none are successful until he appears as Old Mam's long-dead love, Willy. Death is no longer implacable, but subtle, and his sum-mons is open to negotiation. Old Mam does not give in until she has been promised the return of a day of her youth, and the favor of sleeping next to her lover for eternity.

An interesting variation on the above story, in which an old woman confronts the lover of her youth, is found in "The

Tombling Day." While helping to move coffins from an old graveyard to a new one, Grandma Loblilly opens the box containing the body of her lover of sixty years before. The body has been perfectly preserved, and at first Grandma is dismayed at the comparison between his youth and her age. But when the body suddenly disintegrates, Grandma's eyes are cleared. Wisest of the three old ladies, she doesn't bother to reject death, but instead reaffirms her embrace on life: "I'm young! I'm eighty, but I'm younger'n *him*! . . . I'm younger'n *all* the dead ones in the whole world!"

This high-spirited attitude in the face of death is an important one to Bradbury. It figures significantly in the novel *Something Wicked This Way Comes* as exemplified by one of the epigraphs chosen for that book, a quote from *Moby Dick* in which Stubb says, "I know not all that be coming, but be it what it will, I'll go to it laughing."

One of the traditional Halloween representations of Death is as the Grim Reaper. Bradbury takes this personification literally in the fantasy "The Scythe." This story of a poor man and his family who take over a farm from a dying man, could easily descend into allegory, but never does. Drew discovers slowly, and in a matter-of-fact way that he has taken over Death's job, and that every stalk of wheat he cuts marks the end of a human life. Drew struggles with his role several times, but eventually reconciles himself to making his living being Death.

Juan Diaz also uses death to support his family in "The Lifework of Juan Diaz," save that he supports his family by *being* dead. Juan's wife steals his mummified remains from the graveyard and sets them up in her home as a tourist attraction. As a result, Juan is able to support his family better in death than he did in life.

We encounter death as a kind of life-style in "The Dead Man." Here, Odd Martin, the town lunatic, insists that he is dead, finally finds a woman to share his conviction, marries her, and is last seen traveling with his bride toward the cemetery. This image of death as a state of mind is explored in a less macabre way in two stories. "Jack-in-the-Box" ends with young Edwin gladly embracing the "death" of the outside world his mother had been shielding him from. In "The Wonderful Death of Dudley Stone," a famous writer is confronted by a jealous rival who intends to kill him. Stone agrees to "die" by simply not writing any more books. The rival is satisfied, and Stone, through his "death" is able to relax and enjoy life for the first time.

In these lighter stories, we may get the feeling that death is being bandied about a bit. Bradbury seems to be holding death at arm's length, reducing it to an abstraction, a concept, a delusion, a fantasy. In so doing, he provides an out for himself, a means of transcending death in stories in which there is no implied hope of immortality among the stars.

the pandemonium shadow show

Monsters • Misfits • Madmen

Monsters

■ Monsters have a venerable heritage in fiction. The cyclops, the Minotaur, Grendel, fairy tale dragons, a host of strange beasts populate myth and literature through the ages. If one is given to psychological interpretation, monsters may be taken to represent the negative aspects of the human mind externalized and made larger than life. Raw fear, and the impulse toward rape, theft, or destruction are externalized and invested in an ugly and gigantic figure. A knight in armor, or other suitable hero, is then sent to battle this figure and, in defeating it, symbolically defeats the worst in human nature. On a more practical level, the monster can provide the storyteller with an easy source of action and excitement. In modern times, with more psychological sophistication, monsters have become more subtle, and huge size is no longer a prerequisite.

Ray Bradbury's monsters come in many shapes and sizes. Interestingly, his monsters that resemble the lizard or snake-like fairy tale dragons are his most sympathetic. It is as if Bradbury was at least subconsciously aware of their historical role as scapegoats for human failings, and sought to even the score a bit. Bradbury was certainly influenced by the monster movies he enjoyed as a child—particularly "King Kong." The love Bradbury has for "King Kong"—which he claims to have seen forty-three times in forty-two years—probably arises, at least in part, from the qualities the film shares with his own best work: technical finesse, a tightly organized structure, intense evocation of mood, and an enthusiastic celebration of primitive emotions. Kong is something of a tragic figure, doomed not only by his love for the woman he discovers, but also by his inability to adapt to the modern world. This element of being not only in the wrong place but also in the wrong *time* runs through all three of Bradbury's dragon-monster stories.

Most fearsome of Bradbury's dragons is the *Tyrannosaurus rex* in "A Sound of Thunder." This is about as close as Bradbury comes to the monster as rampaging beast. Still, the dinosaur is basically an innocent creature, the intended victim of hunter Eckels' search for the ultimate game. When the beast appears "with a gliding ballet step, far too poised and balanced for its ten tons," Eckels is properly terrified: "My God! . . . It could reach up and grab the moon!" In the end, however, the dinosaur turns out to have been less monstrous in its effect than Eckels himself, for when the hunting party returns to its own time, it finds the world horribly changed because of a butterfly crushed when Eckels fled in panic.

Probably the most famous of Bradbury's dragons is the sea serpent from "The Fog Horn." Bradbury recalls how he was walking with his wife along the Pacific shore one day when he noticed the serpentine ruins of a rollercoaster in an abandoned amusement park. The ruins suggested the body of a dinosaur to him, an image he later remembered while listening to a lonely fog horn off Santa Monica. Bradbury dashed the story off in a single day, then submitted it to *The Saturday Evening Post*, where it was soon accepted. Published under the title

"The Beast from 20,000 Fathoms," the story was one of Bradbury's earliest breaks into a major national magazine. "The Fog Horn" introduces another vividly described dragon monster: ". . . From the surface of the cold sea came a head, a large head, dark-colored, with immense eyes, and then a neck. And then—not a body—but more neck and more! The head rose a full forty feet above the water on a slender and beautiful dark neck. Only then did the body, like a little island of black coral and shells and crayfish, drip up from the subterranean." This is Bradbury's saddest monster. It is the last of its kind, lured by the fog horn it mistakenly takes for the call of another of its species. The creature is truly lost in time, and the two lighthouse keepers who witness its arrival are as saddened as they are terrified. One of the men reflects upon what life has been like for the monster: "I saw it all . . . the million years of waiting alone . . . the million years of isolation at the bottom of the sea, the insanity of time there, while the sky cleared of reptile birds, the swamps dried on the continental lands, the sloths and saber-tooths had their day and sank in tar pits, and men ran like white ants upon the hills."

"The Dragon" starts off as a monster story, but ends up as a twist on Bradbury's theme of reality as determined by point of view. Two knights in armor and the crew of a modern locomotive confront each other from what each regards as the real world. In this case, both man and "monster" are lost in time. Life is no longer the issue, but rather the survival of one or the other's view of reality. In this light, the story has similarities to the chapter "Night Meeting" in *The Martian Chronicles*.

Bradbury's scariest monsters are not lizards or dinosaurs or any other hulking beast. They are shapeless, invisible, yet powerful beings which, because of their incomprehensible form are more apt as metaphors for human fears and passions than any flesh and blood animal. The first such creature appears in "The Wind." One December evening, Herb Thompson gets a phone call from his friend Allin. Allin claims he is being teased by the wind. "It comes in the window and blows the curtains a little bit. Just enough to tell me." It develops that Allin has been unfortunate enough to discover that the winds of the world are alive and intelligent, and that they gather to plan their mischief in a remote valley in the Himalayas. Allin obviously knows too much, and the wind is out to get him. The wind is a superb metaphor for paranoia; powerful, pervasive and impossible to escape. To set off this enormous monster, Bradbury tells the story from a restricted viewpoint. The scene of the story never leaves Thompson's home, and we learn what the wind is doing only through the increasingly frantic phone calls from Allin. Thompson's wife, skeptical and annoyed by the phone calls, pressures her husband not to answer, or to keep the calls short. We are forced to sit through a maddeningly quiet evening of cards with the Thompsons and their friends while wondering what is going on over at Allin's. During one of Allin's last phone calls, Thompson thinks he hears many other voices on the line. When he asks his friend about this, Allin replies:

> That? . . . Those are the voices of twelve thousand killed in a typhoon, seven thousand killed by a hurricane, three thousand buried by a cyclone. Am I boring you? That's what the wind is. It's a lot of people dead. The wind killed them, took their minds to give itself intelligence. It took all their voices and made them into one voice. All those millions of people killed in the past ten thousand years, tortured and run from continent to continent on the backs and in the bellies of monsoons and whirlwinds. Oh Christ, what a poem you could write about it!

Although Allin lives nearby, there is, of course, no point in Thompson going to his aid, since the wind can disappear instantly to return later. By keeping Thompson on the phone, listening as Allin's house is torn apart by the wind, Bradbury underlines the impotence Thompson faces—and would face, even if Allin's problems were entirely within his own mind.

A monster that can be seen as the embodiment of raw possessiveness appears in "The Women." While one woman suns herself on the beach next to her husband, her monstrous counterpart rises from the depths of the sea:

> It was as if a light came on in a green room . . . Out of the depths it came, indolently. A shell, a wisp, a bubble, a weed, a glitter, a whisper, a gill. Suspended in its depths were brainlike trees of frosted coral, eyelike pips of yellow kelp, hairlike fluids of weed. Growing with the tides, growing with the ages, collecting and hoarding and saving unto itself identities and ancient dusts, octupus-inks and all the trivia of the sea.

The creature does not know human love, it only feels a desire to possess, to try the man out like a toy. When the monster approaches the beach, the wife begins to sense something is wrong, and a subtle, almost subconscious struggle begins to take place between them. The sea creature has no power on land, so it must use cunning to lure the man into the water. This it does by working to undermine the relationship between the man and his wife in small, apparently trivial, ways:

> She felt his arm tense and relax, tense and relax.
> "Dammit," he said. "There it is again."
> They both sat listening.
> "I don't hear anything—"
> "Shh!" he cried. "For god's sake—"
> The waves broke on the shore, silent mirrors, heaps of melting, whispering glass.
> "Somebody singing."
> "What?"
> "I'd swear it was someone singing."
> "Nonsense."
> "No. Listen."
> They did that for a while.
> "I don't hear a thing," she said, turning very cold.

The wife is forced to play a cunning game, too, since direct conflict with the creature is impossible. The woman realizes that her continued possession of her husband depends upon his not going into the water. In this battle, the man plays an insignificant, pawn-like role. At one point, the wife sends her husband off on some trumped-up errand, then takes the opportunity to walk to the water's edge and confront her adversary:

> You can't have him, she thought. Whoever or whatever you are, he's mine and you can't have him. I don't know what's going on; I don't know anything, really. All I know is we're going on a train tonight at seven. And we won't be here tomorrow. So you can just stay here and wait, ocean, sea, or whatever it is that's wrong here today.

The third and most dangerous of Bradbury's amorphous monsters is the creature in "The One Who Waits." The scene is the planet Mars. In an ancient stone well, a strange being introduces itself:

> I live in a well. I live like smoke in the well. Like vapor in a stone throat . . . I am mist and moonlight and memory . . . I wait in cool silence and there will be a day when I no longer wait.

Presently a rocket lands near the well. Some men get out, begin exploring, and eventually gather around the well to test the water. This is the moment the creature has been waiting for. In the twinkling of an eye, the monster takes over the bodies of Jones first, then the rest of the crew. Like the wind, this creature seems to be some sort of natural force. But unlike the wind it has no cunning or willful cruelty. Still it is no less destructive. At first the creature enjoys the new sensations it can experience through possession of a physical body:

> It is good to do several things after ten thousand years. It is good to breathe the air and it is good to feel the sun in the flesh deep and going deeper and it is good to feel the structure of ivory, the fine skeleton hidden in the warming flesh, and it is good to hear sounds clearer

and more immediate than they were in the stone deepness of a well. I sit enchanted.

But as the men begin to resist it, it kills them off one by one. There is no malice in this, the creature is just a blind, amoral force behaving according to its own rules. As an unreasoning, blind force, it perhaps most suitably represents man's fear and rage in the abstract. It is an interesting turnabout to have a monster representing destructive fear leap back into human minds to wreak its havoc.

Misfits

Misfits are monsters on a more human scale, monstrous not because they are huge or beastly, but because they are ugly, lonely, frightening or social outcasts. As with beauty, monstrosity seems to be in the eyes of the beholder.

The image of the misfit is a common one in the world of fantasy and science fiction. In Bradbury's fiction dealing with his youth, and in some of his personal recollections, are echoes of a time when he himself was an outsider. Bradbury recalls being scoffed at for his interest in fantastic literature as a child, and ridiculed for his desire to write science fiction. The influence of such experiences upon Bradbury's later writing may be open to question, but there is no doubt that he writes about outsiders with a sympathetic and perceptive eye.

The child as outsider is particularly appropriate in the context of a family drama, and "Homecoming" is an affecting exaggeration of this theme. Timothy is the only normal child in a family of monsters. It is near Halloween, and members of his extended family are converging from all over the world upon his parents' home for the celebration. Timothy's relatives are a charming collection of vampires, witches, werewolves, goblins and demons. The impending festivities only encourage Timothy to muse upon his abnormalities: "Did he sleep in the wonderful polished boxes like the others? He did not! Mother let him have his own bed, his own room, his own mirror. No wonder the family skirted him like a holy man's crucifix." Most of Timothy's relatives treat him with condescension, amusement, or pity. Horrible cousin Leonard makes fun of Timothy because he is afraid of the dark. Nobody can understand why Timothy doesn't like the taste of blood. There are a few bright moments at the party when Uncle Einar, a seven-foot giant with great batwings growing from his shoulders, tosses Timothy about the room so he can sample the exhilaration of flight. But it is the boy's curse to be human and mortal, and even his mother can offer him only the grim consolation that when he dies, ". . . you'll lie at ease forever . . . and I'll come visit every Allhallows Eve and tuck you in the more secure."

Uncle Einar gets a taste of Timothy's predicament in a story of his own. Flying back from a family homecoming, Uncle Einar runs into a high-tension wire and crashes into a meadow in the Illinois countryside. He is found the next morning by Brunilla, the young woman who owns the property. She too is a misfit. "I live alone . . . for, as you see, I'm quite ugly." Brunilla takes Einar back to her farmhouse and nurses him back to health. Most of Einar's faculties return, save for his ability to navigate in the dark. Since he obviously cannot be seen flying in daylight, he is marooned on Brunilla's farm. The odd qualities that separate them from society bring Einar and Brunilla close together, and they eventually marry in secret. Monster and misfit take consolation and strength from each other, and the peculiarities that set them apart from their fellow men become sources of joy to each other. Einar takes Brunilla for an ecstatic nuptial flight high over the Illinois countryside. Brunilla charms Einar with her kindness and alters the furniture so that a winged man can sit in it comfortably.

> "We're in our cocoons, all of us. See how ugly I am?" says Brunilla. "But one day I'll break out, spread wings as fine and handsome as you."
> "You broke out long ago." [Einar replies.]

The couple has four children—all normal looking—and is quite happy. The only problem remaining is Uncle Einar's inability to chance flying in the daytime. Finally he settles upon a clever disguise and, in the happy ending to this story, is able to resume daylight flights by posing as his childrens' kite.

For the misfit (or monster) to find a companion is a rare stroke of luck, as is being able to pass among "normal" people in a successful disguise. Most such creatures are condemned to remain in hiding, or to continually flee to avoid exposure. Willie, in "Hail and Farewell," is a misfit of this latter sort. Willie outwardly appears to be a healthy twelve-year-old boy. He is loved by his parents and popular with his schoolmates. But Willie was adopted by his current parents three years ago, and as the story opens, he is leaving them to seek new parents in another town. For Willie has a secret which, once it becomes generally known, will render him monstrous in the eyes of his family and friends. The secret is simple: Willie is blessed with eternal youth, or close to it, and though Willie retains all of the physical characteristics of a twelve-year-old boy, he is actually over forty years old. Every few years he must move to a new town, find a couple who wants to adopt him, and live with them until it is time to move on again. And that time always comes:

> I tried to stay on once after people began to suspect. "How horrible!" people said. "All these years, playing with our innocent children," they said, "and us not guessing! Awful!" they said. And finally I had to just leave town one night.

Willie is a monstrosity because time is continually passing him by, and he must periodically reinsert himself into a time frame in which he can belong.

In spite of the stress of movings and partings, however, Willie has come to terms with his abnormality. He does not look bizarre enough to become a sideshow freak, but still he becomes a professional of sorts:

One day I saw this man in a restaurant looking at another man's pictures of his children. "Sure wish I had kids," he said. . . . At that very instant I knew what my job would be for all the rest of my life. There *was* work for me, after all. Making lonely people happy. . . . All I had to do was be a mother's son and a father's pride.

There is no such relief for the more traditionally malformed creature in "The Dwarf." At night the dwarf comes to the MIRROR MAZE at the carnival. Fleeing from himself and the world, he stands before the distorting mirror that makes him look tall and thin. Unknowingly, the dwarf serves as a catalyst for the conflicts between two of the carnival staff, Aimee and Ralph. Ralph, who manages the maze, is cruel and boorish, and he becomes increasingly irritated by Aimee's sympathy for the dwarf. One day, Ralph replaces the mirror the dwarf favors with one that makes him look even more disfigured. The dwarf runs in horror, apparently bent on suicide. Aimee rushes after him, but before she does so, she causes Ralph to confront his own monstrosity in the mirror:

> He scowled at the blazing mirror.
> A horrid, ugly little man, two feet high, with a pale, squashed face under an ancient straw hat, scowled back at him. Ralph stood there glaring at himself, his hands at his sides.

Bradbury seems to suggest that Timothy, Uncle Einar, young Willie, and the dwarf are misfits or monsters of circumstance. They are not inherently terrible or frightening, but become so when accidents of time, shape, or size render them aliens in their own world. In most of these cases it is up to the "monster" to adapt or be destroyed. "Tomorrow's Child" presents a different resolution to the problem. Something goes wrong with a new-fangled maternity-assistance machine, and poor Polly Ann gives birth to a seven-pound, eight-ounce blue pyramid. "Your baby," the doctor explains, "was born into—another dimension." Polly and her husband Peter bring their little monster home and attempt to raise it in seclusion. But this doesn't work very well, and the "child" takes its toll on their marriage and sanity. Finally, they are told that though there is no hope of bringing the child back into this dimension, they, the parents, may be sent to join their baby in his dimension. Mother, father, and child will then appear normal to each other, but will appear as monstrosities to the "normal" world. Love solves the problems of identity and alienation that plagued the other outsiders, and when last seen a White Oblong, a slim White Rectangle, and a small Blue Pyramid are playing happily together.

Madmen

A madman is a monster turned outside in. Though he may not differ outwardly from his fellow men, he may still perceive himself stranded in an alien and hostile world, or feel compelled to create a world of his own fantasy. The characteristics of intense fixation, distortion of perception, suppression of important details, or magnification of trivialities are ideal subjects for sensory imagery such as Bradbury's.

Not all of Bradbury's madmen are psychopathic. Some suffer from a gentle madness. The old man in "A Time of Going Away" feels his end is near and prepares to leave his wife and home to seek a place to die—just like some south sea natives he read about in *National Geographic*. His wife, a practical soul, is used to the perverse effect certain periodicals have on him. "Those *Geographic* and *Popular Mechanics* publishers should be forced to see all the half-finished rowboats, helicopters, and one-man batwing gliders in our attic, garage, and cellar," she snorts. She is wise enough to let her husband leave the house, knowing he'll be back when he gets hungry. In the meantime, she burns his copies of *National Geographic*.

A similar let-the-fit-take-its-course policy is adopted by a film producer and director when their star gets a little carried away with his role as Hitler in "Darling Adolf." The actor eventually becomes himself again, but some of Bradbury's other characters who assume new identities never do revert to their true selves. In "Any Friend of Nicholas Nickleby's is a Friend of Mine," a man arrives at the roominghouse run by Ralph Spaulding's grandparents and identifies himself as Charles Dickens. As it turns out, the man always wanted to be a writer, but, never having been able to write very well, finally abandoned his own identity and assumed that of Dickens. He now makes his living travelling about the country giving lectures, while "writing" all of Dickens' novels again from memory. Rather than dissuade the man, Spaulding encourages him, and even engineers a happy ending wherein "Dickens" runs off with the Green Town librarian who always wanted to be Emily Dickinson. (The theme of books committed to and then recalled from memory is explored more fully in *Fahrenheit 451*.) Finally, in the story "Henry the Ninth," the lone man left in England after the entire population has moved to warmer climes, dubs himself Henry IX, the last king of England, and wanders about the deserted country keeping its memories alive.

"Jack-in-the-Box" represents one of Bradbury's more serious stories of madness. Edwin is raised in a large mansion by his mother, a woman apparently deranged since the death of her husband some years before. Edwin has never been outside of the house except for visits to the small back garden. He yearns to burst free from his confined world, and the jack-in-the-box is the symbol of this for him. But his mother has warned him that, as it was for his father, the outside world is Death.

This story is one of Bradbury's more interesting excursions into the world of split personalities. Edwin knows two women: his mother, with whom he spends most of his time, and his teacher, who greets him in a classroom on the second floor. What he does not know is that his mother is also the teacher, that she uses makeup, glasses, and a cowled costume to disguise herself in the classroom. Bradbury guides us through the story from Edwin's viewpoint as he gradually discovers the truth about his mother. The house, and the various rooms that are opened to the boy, becomes a symbol of both his awakening and of the compulsively ordered fantasy world of his mother. When his mother dies unexpectedly, Edwin makes his break for the world outside. The extent to which his mother's disordered view of the world has impressed itself upon Edwin is revealed as he dashes about the streets touching all the things he's never seen before and shouting, "I'm dead, I'm dead, I'm glad I'm dead . . . it's *good* to be dead!"

The ventriloquist in "And So Died Riabouchinska" is more traditionally schizophrenic. The puzzle in this case is not to find out what is going on in the outside world, but to discover what is happening in the private world of Fabian's mind. As with Edwin's mother and teacher, Fabian and his dummy have but one soul—yet in Fabian's case the question is: who has it?

Bradbury rarely goes into the causes of madness, but in two stories hot weather seems the significant factor. In "The Burning Man," Douglas (Spaulding?) and his Aunt Neva are out driving in the country one hot July day when they stop to give a man a lift. The man personifies the oppressive heat of the sun even as he seems terror stricken by it: "Get going. It's *after* us! The sun, I mean, of course! . . . Git! Or we'll *all* go mad!"

The power of heat to cause madness, even if temporary, is further explored in "Touched with Fire." This intriguing story is obviously fiction, yet seems based on fact. It involves two retired insurance salesmen who have made a study of the relationship between weather conditions and violent crimes. Their task is to save a woman whose foul temper, combined with a high temperature-humidity-index, seems likely to provoke her husband into a murderous rage.

The causes of madness are irrelevant in stories of sheer horror or suspense. We do not know why Mr. Greppin in "The Smiling People" is so intent on having silence. What is shown, however, are some of the fanatical lengths to which he goes to insure it in the house—even to stilling the pendulum on the grandfather's clock. In the dining room, four of his relatives sit in absolute silence, as they have since the night Greppin grew furious at their criticisms of him and slit their throats. Now Greppin walks the hushed rooms alone while the others sit with their dreadful ear-to-ear smiles. Bradbury's vivid descriptions fully convey the strange intensity of Greppin's fascination with silence:

> There are silences and silences. Each with its own identity. There were summer night silences, which weren't silences at all, but layer on layer of insect chorals and the sound of electric lamps swaying in lonely small orbits on lonely country roads, casting out feeble rings of illumination upon which the night fed—summer night silence which, to be a silence, demanded an indolence and a neglect and an indifference upon the part of the listener. . . . And there was a winter silence, but it was an encoffined silence, ready to burst free at the first nod of spring . . .

Paranoia as well as obsession is subject matter for the suspense or horror story. Mr. Howard of "Let's Play 'Poison' " hates children and is convinced that they all hate him. The games they play in the street in front of his house are intended simply to annoy him. His obsession causes him panic, and his panic makes him careless. The children do very little to bring about his end; paranoia is his undoing.

Sometimes paranoia is quite justified, as in the case of Mr. Spallner, who discovers that the same crowd always gathers at the scene of accidents in his city, and that the way the crowd behaves toward the injured determines whether or not they survive. Of course, he knows too much, and shortly thereafter his car is rammed by a truck. The crowd gathers and familiar faces look down at him. "Is—is he dead?" asks one of them. "No. Not yet. But he will be dead before the ambulance arrives."

Most of Bradbury's madmen, like his misfits, can be understood in terms of "normal" values. Their needs and fears are,
in most cases, simply exaggerations or distortions of needs and
fears common to many people. In "The Cistern," however,
Bradbury sets himself an interesting challenge, to generate
understanding and a certain amount of sympathy for someone
whose obsession is alien, to say the least. As the story opens, two
sisters are at home on a rainy afternoon. Anna is caught up in a
fantasy about the cistern system under the streets:

> Wouldn't it be fun—I mean, very secret? To live in the
> cistern and peek up at people through the slots and see
> them and them not see you? Like when you were a child
> and played hide-and-seek and nobody found you, and
> there you were in their midst all the time, all sheltered
> and hidden and warm and excited. I'd like that. That's
> what it must be like to live in the cistern.

Anna describes a dream she has had in which two lovers
meet and dwell with each other in the cisterns. During dry
periods, they "lie in little hidden niches, like those Japanese
water flowers, all dry and compact and old and quiet."

When Anna's sister Juliet challenges the possibility of two
people being able to live in a cistern, Anna replies, "Did I say
they were alive? . . . Oh, but no. They're dead." Like Willie in
"Hail and Farewell" and the Dwarf, Anna seeks the tranquility
of living life according to her own vision. Anna's mental state
renders her as alien in her world as Willie and the Dwarf are in
theirs. But we cannot sympathize with Anna's solution to her
alienness—only with her need to seek out a solution. In this
story, Bradbury has produced a laboratory experiment in
which Anna's fantasy can be examined as an abstract
phenomenon. Bradbury's touch is as light here as it is chilling.
When Anna leaves to follow her dream, our reaction is an
intriguing mixture of repugnance and understanding.

Anna finds peace in following her impulse, but when Acton
in "The Fruit at the Bottom of the Bowl" follows his impulse,

he finds only frenzy. Acton's impulse is to murder Huxley. Having accomplished this, Acton is gradually overcome with guilt and fears discovery. "The Fruit at the Bottom of the Bowl" is a beautifully balanced variation of what might be called the Lady Macbeth syndrome. In his efforts to cover up his crime, Acton becomes aware of his fingerprints impressed everywhere in Huxley's house. He begins to see his fingerprints resemble spider webs, and: "when his back was turned the little spiders came out of the woodwork and delicately spun their fragile little half-invisible webs." The pace of the story is brisk and intense, we are given no time to dwell upon its improbabilities. Rarely has compulsive cleanliness been so fiendishly entertaining.

future imperfect

Space Travel • Other Planets
Time Travel • The End of the World

Space Travel

■ Space travel is an element in Ray Bradbury's work which has attained mythic significance. For Bradbury, space is not merely a stage upon which stories of the future are played, it is what the Great Plains were to the pioneers; not just a frontier but a symbol of the future for the human race. Many of Bradbury's ideas about space culminate in *The Martian Chronicles,* but actually, Mars is just a way station, a place for humanity to catch its breath before stepping off to the stars. Man's final independence of Earth or of any single planet or solar system is the key to immortality, as Bradbury sees it. This is an expansive concept, and somewhat unwieldy within the context of short fiction, and Bradbury does little more than touch upon it in any given story. In some of his poems, Bradbury is able to express the myth directly, but in his stories he tends to reveal fragments of the grand plan through the perspective of individual human beings. There are the dreamers, the planners, the spectators, and of course the pioneers—the spacemen themselves. One of the dreamers is Fiorello Bodoni of "The Rocket," who cannot pass on the experience, but can at least pass on the dream, by rigging up a mock-up rocket electronically to produce a simulated ride through space for his family.

For some, the dream of space is a threat to the comfort and safety of old ideas. In "The Machineries of Joy," a Catholic priest chafes at the idea that we might learn something from space travel:

> Learn what? That most of the things we've taught in the past on Earth don't fit out there on Mars or Venus or Wherever in hell Vittorini would push us? Drive Adam and Eve out of some new Garden, on Jupiter, with our very own rocket fires? Or worse, find there's no Eden, no Adam, no Eve, no damned Apple nor Serpent, no Fall, no Original Sin, no Annunciation, no Birth, no Son, you go on with the list, no nothing at all! on one blasted world tailing another? Is *that* what we must learn?

But Bradbury seems most sympathetic to characters who appreciate space travel as a step on a path leading from a past of dreams toward a future reality. There is the Captain of the space ship *Copa de Oro*—"Cup of Gold"—who, as his ship is about to complete its astonishing mission of scooping up a piece of the sun, muses about a similar scene from the past:

> A million years ago a naked man on a lonely northern trail saw lightning strike a tree. And while his clan fled, with bare hands he plucked a limb of fire, broiling the flesh of his fingers, to carry it, running in triumph, shielding it from the rain with his body, to his cave, where he shrieked out a laugh and teased it full on a mound of leaves and gave his people summer.

And there is Jedediah Prentiss who, on the eve of his piloting the first rocket to the moon, mentally renames himself after former pioneers of flight, and composes his own fanciful epitaph:

Icarus Montgolfier Wright.

Born: nine hundred years before Christ.

Grammar school: Paris, 1783. High school, college: Kitty Hawk, 1903. Graduation from Earth to Moon: this day, God willing, August 1, 1970. Death and burial, with luck on Mars, summer 1999 in the Year of Our Lord.

At the core of the space travel experience, then, is what it means, not just on a cosmic level, but to the individuals involved. Not just Bradbury's rocket captains, but spectators and humbler pioneers appreciate this meaning. As the father and mother of a rocket pilot sit on their front porch and search the horizon for the liftoff of their son's ship, the father muses, "It's really the end of the beginning. The Stone Age, Bronze Age, Iron Age; from now on we'll lump all those together under one big name for when we walked on Earth and heard the birds at morning and cried with envy." Bradbury's common people feel a tie then with the past, and are conscious of the repetitions which new voyages toward new frontiers bring. And Bradbury's space voyagers are common people. In this they vary considerably from the sort of person involved in actual space travel so far. Perhaps it is only a matter of time before space travel becomes cheap and practical enough to be considered by the average person. But Bradbury is not directly concerned with this issue. For him, space travel represents a development of humanity as a whole, regardless of how exclusive the fraternity of astronauts and space scientists has come to be. His stories are not so much literal predictions as they are translations of what must be highly technological space programs into familiar mythic terms. A young woman in the story "The Wilderness" asks herself a question as she awaits the rocket which will take her to Mars to begin a new life as a pioneer wife:

Is this how it was over a century ago . . . when the women, the night before, lay ready for sleep, or not ready, in the small towns of the East, and heard the

sound of horses in the night and the creak of the Cones-
toga wagons ready to go, and the brooding of oxen
under the trees, and the cry of children already lonely
before their time?. . . On the rim of the precipice, on the
edge of the cliff of stars. In their time the smell of
buffalo, and in our time the smell of the Rocket. Is this,
then, how it was?

The answer may be rhetorical, but—at least as far as Bradbury is concerned—does not change significantly even if the
actual population of Mars is accomplished one day by shipping
female ova in the wombs of sheep to be later fertilized with
frozen sperm.

Bradbury devotes a few stories to the first space travelers,
but writes mainly about space travel as an established fact.
"The Rocket Man" takes place at a time when rocket piloting is
a common, if dangerous, job. Space, it seems, can get into a
man's blood the way the sea did in ages past. The man's wife
wants him to give up his job before he is killed, but her words
fall on deaf ears. Doug, the man's son, is himself caught up with
the romance of space as he examines his father's luggage:

> From the opened case spilled his black uniform, like a
> black nebula, stars glittering here or there, distantly, in
> the material. I kneaded the dark stuff in my warm
> hands; I smelled the planet Mars, an iron smell, and the
> planet Venus, a green ivy smell, and the planet Mercury,
> a scent of sulphur and fire; and I could smell the milky
> moon and the hardness of stars.

This childlike wonder and fascination with space travel is a
constant thread in Bradbury's stories. And indeed, for children, space can be a wonderful place, as it is for the young boy
whose Christmas present during his first space flight is a
glimpse out the rocket's giant porthole "out into space and the
deep night at the burning and the burning of ten billion billion
white and lovely candles. . . ." But for adults, space can also be
a place of madness and death.

The Rocket Man ignores his wife's pleas to give up his job, and on his next flight dies when his ship falls into the sun. The extent to which space can distort traditional symbols in ways the sea never could is suggested in the passage reflecting the reaction to the man's death of the mother and son:

> For a long time after my father died my mother slept through the days and wouldn't go out. We had breakfast at midnight and lunch at three in the morning, and dinner at the cold dim hour of 6 A.M. We went to all-night shows and went to bed at sunrise.

For Bradbury, space, like the sea, can put man to severe tests; it can find his weakness and work away at it until he overcomes it or is destroyed by it. Hitchcock in "No Particular Night or Morning" suffers from a crucial weakness. He only believes in what is right in front of him at the moment. "When I'm in Boston, New York is dead. When I'm in New York, Boston is dead. When I don't see a man for a day, he's dead." Hitchcock's main problem, Bradbury seems to say, is that he has no imagination. And imagination is, for Bradbury, what allows us to connect one reality with another in a meaningful way. "No Particular Night or Morning" is an allegory on the value of imagination. Hitchcock is in constant conflict with Clemens, a fellow crewman on a ship a billion miles out in space. In the vast sea of literal and metaphorical nothingness, Clemens' imagination links him with his past and keeps him sane: " 'I'm putting a dime in the phone slot right now,' he said, pantomiming it with a slow smile. 'And calling my girl in Evanston. Hello, Barbara!' "

Attempts are made to save Hitchcock from his increasing fixation on the void of space, but to no avail. When Hitchcock finally climbs into a space suit and steps out of the ship, his voice can be heard over the radio as the void of his imagination merges into the void around him.

No hands . . . I haven't any hands any more. Never had any. No lips. No face. No head. Nothing. Only space. Only space. . ."

Hitchcock's predicament, the mind floating helplessly in the void, is echoed a dozenfold in "Kaleidoscope." A rocket explodes and flings its crew "like a dozen wriggling silverfish" off into space in all directions. Alone, each man has contact with the others only through the radio in his spacesuit. In spite of the fragmented circumstances, Bradbury maintains a tight dramatic unity to the story. First, the title recalls how the single image in a kaleidoscope is produced by hundreds of jagged fragments. Then, as the men contact one another we are told that "space began to weave its strange voices in and out, on a great dark loom, crossing, recrossing, and making a final pattern." And finally, at the story's end, the crew of the ship is likened to a brain which is disintegrating—"and as a body dies when the brain ceases functioning, so the spirit of the ship and their long time together and what they meant to one another was dying." Aside from these images, all the crewmen share a common attempt—modified by bitterness, remorse, or resignation—to find meaning in their lives at the end. Hollis has little success at this and is still concerned about it when his body enters Earth's atmosphere to burn up like a shooting star. In a rather sourly ironic ending, Bradbury has Hollis transcend his fate by bringing a moment of delight and beauty to a boy and his mother.

Bradbury returns to the theme of the castaway in space a third, and less successful time in "G.B.S.—Mark V." Charles Willis spends his time conversing with a robot replica of George Bernard Shaw, while his fellow crewmen aboard a long-traveling spaceship cavort with robot women. When the ship is destroyed by a meteor, Willis and the robot are flung off into space. Willis takes consolation from his battery-powered fellow-castaway, but, this is not entirely convincing. The story does avoid a cloyingly happy ending by leaving the ultimate fate of the pair in some doubt.

Other Planets

Bradbury is most famous for his stories about Mars, but he has written a few stories about worlds other than Mars or Earth. There is the Eden-like "planet 7 of star system 84" in "Here There Be Tygers." The planet is so seductively beautiful that the captain of the exploratory rocket which lands there comments, "If ever a planet was a woman, this one is." The story is an old-fashioned exploration of a mysterious world tale of the sort quite common to science fiction magazines of the forties and fifties. The planet is Mother Nature personified, and the story lightly treats ecological themes. Villain of the piece is Chatterton, who states his philosophy bluntly: "You have to beat a planet at its own game. . . . Get in and rip it up, kill its snakes, poison its animals, dam its rivers, sow its fields, depollinate its air, mine it, nail it down, hack away at it, and get the blazes out from under when you have what you want." Fortunately, unlike our own Earth, this planet can take care of itself. Chatterton comes to a suitably grisly end, and the good natured rocket crew departs, vowing to keep the location of the planet secret. One crewman is left behind to live happily ever after. He is Driscoll—apparently from a family of nature lovers, since Bradbury casts another Driscoll (Benjamin) as a futuristic Johnny Appleseed in *The Martian Chronicles*.

"Frost and Fire" takes us to a somewhat more interesting world, unnamed, but apparently the planet Mercury. Here, settlers from the first Earth expeditions have evolved into beings whose metabolisms have so accelerated due to the intolerable climate that they live out their entire lifespans in just eight days. The story is a cliffhanger about two of the beings who attempt to reach a long abandoned space ship, with its promise of a return to a life which, to them, seems eternal.

There are two stories about Venus which Bradbury pictures as a jungle world enveloped in perpetual rain and fog. One is a story of cruelty, "All Summer in a Day," in which a little girl is locked in a closet by her classmates on the one day in seven years when the sun comes out. The other, "The Long Rain," is about the crew of a wrecked rocket seeking shelter from the eternal, maddening downpour. Bradbury's Venus is no more scientifically accurate than his Mars. But, as with the red planet, Bradbury's powers of description make it real enough. The rain of Venus, he tells us, ". . . was a mizzle, a downpour, a fountain, a whipping at the eyes, an undertow at the ankles; it was a rain to drown all rains and the memory of rains. It came by the pound and the ton, it hacked at the jungle and cut the trees like scissors and shaved the grass and tunneled the soil and molted the bushes. It shrank men's hands into the hands of wrinkled apes . . ." After Mars, Venus is Bradbury's most richly realized world. It seems regrettable that the hostility of the climate seems to have precluded further human endeavor there.

Time Travel

Bradbury's stories about time travel are more restrictive than those about space travel. The motivation of the voyagers is significantly different. The space traveller is plunging into the unknown, prepared for the unexpected, seeking something new. Bradbury's time travellers, on the other hand, tend to visit a specific time with a specific purpose in mind. They seek the old and the familiar rather than the new and strange. For these reasons, Bradbury's time travellers are not tempted to follow those of H.G. Wells into the future. The past represents a known territory, mapped by memory and history, and it is in this territory that Bradbury's time travellers wander. (The one exception is in "The Dragon" in which neither knights nor locomotive engineer willingly trespass in the others' time.)

Mr. Finch in "A Scent of Sarsaparilla" seeks the summers of his youth and an escape from the winter which "lay . . . outside forever, a great leaden wine press smashing down its colorless lid of sky . . ." The young couple in "The Fox and the Forest" seek the peaceful beauties of Mexico in 1938, fleeing their own time, 2155 A.D., in which the world had become ". . . a great black ship pulling away from the shore of sanity and civilization . . . taking two billion people with it, whether they wanted to go or not, to death . . . into radioactive flame and madness." And Eckels in "A Sound of Thunder" seeks only the pleasure of shooting the ultimate game, *Tyrannosaurus rex,* alive in its own time, sixty million years ago.

Two time travellers combine questionable taste with an impossible dream and go back to encounter famous writers. Henry William Field in "Forever and the Earth" uses a time machine to whisk Thomas Wolfe from his deathbed into the future, so that Wolfe might write, as only he could, of the wonders of space travel. In "The Kilimanjaro Device," a fan of Ernest Hemingway uses another machine to pick up the famous author just before his suicide and to transport him to a suitable burial site on the slopes of Kilimanjaro. Both stories seem more concerned with the authors' public legends than with the quality of their writing, and so are not very successful. In any case, the idea of using time travel to tidy up history or to experiment with placing the right people in the right place at the right time tends to stretch the credibility of this most unlikely of science fiction voyaging well past the breaking point.

An interesting variation on the time travel theme is to be found in "Night Call, Collect." No actual time travel is involved, but nevertheless, a man succeeds in reaching across a span of fifty years and murdering—himself. Barton is left behind when the colonists from Earth abandon their settlements on Mars. To occupy his time, Barton programs a series of cruel practical jokes into the planet's automatic telephone system. Fifty years later, as Barton wanders about in his old age, the phones begin ringing and his own voice lures him into a series of traps he has long forgotten how to avoid. The story crackles with invention and explores the paradoxes of time travel better than many other stories on the subject.

The End of the World

Since science fiction deals primarily with the future, many science fiction writers have speculated upon the ultimate event of the future: the end of the world. Since the late forties, the threat of atomic annihilation has encouraged few writers to be optimistic about the Earth one day experiencing a natural demise. Bradbury has written a number of stories about the final days of Earth as well as tales depicting the collapse of smaller, more personal worlds.

Most effective of these latter is "Perhaps We Are Going Away," in which a small Indian boy and his grandfather confront the imminent destruction of the world they know following the arrival of the first white men. The man and boy speak to each other through sign language, and the old man describes the fate of the Indian world in terms of a change of season:

> The birds, his hands cried suddenly, are flying south! Summer is over!
> No, the boy's hands said, Summer has just begun! I see no birds!
> They are so high, said the old man's fingers, that only the blind can feel their passage. They shadow the heart more than the earth. I feel them pass south in my blood. Summer goes. We may go with it.

Once again Bradbury uses the metaphor of a change of season to express a change in perception or reality. The metaphor used here suits the Indians, of course, but Bradbury makes it his own many times in such stories as "The Day It Rained Forever" and "Rocket Summer" from *The Martian Chronicles*.

"Almost the End of the World" is a comic variant on the story in which one or two people escape the atomic holocaust by spending the night in a mineshaft. Willy Bersinger and Samuel Fitts roll into Rock Junction, Arizona, after two months of prospecting in the mountains. They are astonished to find the entire population frantically engaged in painting the whole town. Disaster has struck: sunspots have wiped out all television reception, possibly forever, and people all over the country are desperately trying to fill their idle hours. The two prospectors accept the change in the world philosophically:

> "Man survives . . . man endures. Too bad we missed the big change. It must have been a fierce thing, a time of trials and testings. Samuel, I don't recall, do you? What have *we* ever seen on TV?"
> "Saw a woman wrestle a bear two falls out of three, one night."

The people of Oak Lane, California contemplate the destruction of their town in "Yes, We'll Gather at the River." The "river" in this case means the river of traffic which brings life to the town's businesses, and which will be moving over to a new bypass highway the next morning. As with all of his end-of-the-world stories, Bradbury expresses the larger drama in terms of smaller ones. Charlie Moore is reluctant to close his tobacco store in Oak Lane for what may be the last time. But at 9:30 PM "Moore finally touched the wooden Indian's elbow as if disturbing a friend and hating to bother." It is through intimate gestures such as these that Bradbury builds a picture of the drama beyond the horizon of his story. This is just as true in his tales of general destruction of the world.

Most of Bradbury's end-of-the-world stories are told from the viewpoint of a single domestic scene. The disaster is thus expressed through a narrow, personal intensity ideally suited to the short story. The basic domestic unit, the single family, is used several times.

"The Garbage Collector" chillingly explores results of a nuclear war as these could affect a common laborer. A garbage collector comes home to his wife deeply disturbed about a development relating to his job. Bradbury stages the scene between the husband and his wife as an awkward confrontation, the wife not realizing why her husband has been so affected, the husband having trouble articulating his feelings. He suddenly announces that he wants to quit his job, apparently because the city has installed radios in his truck. The wife presses him for details and he begins to explain:

> "After the atomic bombs hit our city, those radios will talk to us. And then our garbage trucks will go pick up the bodies."
> "Well, that seems practical. When—"
> "The garbage trucks," he said, "go out and pick up all the bodies."

The wife begins to appreciate her husband's feelings, but does not like the idea of pulling up stakes and leaving the city:

> She took a deep breath. "Can't we think it over a few more days?"
> "I don't know. I'm afraid of that. I'm afraid if I think it over . . . I'll get used to it. And oh Christ, it just doesn't seem right a man, a human being, should ever let himself get used to any idea like that."

As they speak, the wife goes through her domestic chores, preparing supper. The husband states some of the morbid considerations his imagination has been grappling with, such as "wondering . . . if you put the bodies in the trucks lengthwise or endwise, with the heads on the right, or the *feet* on the right. Men and women together, or separated?" Some of his thoughts cannot even be expressed openly, as when he recalls ". . . how it was late in the day . . . with the truck full and the canvas pulled over the great bulk of garbage. . . . And how it was if you suddenly pulled the canvas back and look in. And for a few seconds you saw the white things like macaroni or noodles, only the white things were alive and boiling up, millions of them."

Elements of horror enter into the mundane domestic situation and are strengthened by the tension between husband and wife in "The Garbage Collector." An entirely different atmosphere prevails in "The Last Night of the World." A husband and wife discuss apocalyptic matters during a quiet evening at home. They and all their acquaintances have had the same dream, that the world is going to end that night. The wife questions her husband on how he envisions the end:

> "A war?"
> He shook his head.
> "Not the hydrogen or atom bomb?"
> "No."
> "Or germ warfare?"
> "None of those at all," he said, stirring his coffee slowly. "But just, let's say, the closing of a book."

The calmness and certainty with which the couple faces their impending fate generates the suspense in this story. One waits for either their fate or their attitude to change. Both people are themselves struck by their reaction to the situation:

> "How can we sit here and talk this way?"
> "Because there's nothing else to do."
> "That's it, of course; for if there were, we'd be doing it. I suppose this is the first time in the history of the world that everyone has known just what they were going to do during the night."

Bradbury never actually allows us to discover whether the couple is right or wrong about the world ending. But the story's conclusion is satisfying nonetheless, since the couple's calm resignation to their fate is so absolute, so transcendental, that it becomes meaningful regardless of what might happen at midnight.

"The Vacation" involves another young couple in a sort of variation on a common theme in fairy tales in which a character makes a foolish wish and suffers the consequences when the wish comes true. One night the young husband says to his wife: "Wouldn't it be nice . . . if we woke tomorrow and everyone in the world was gone and everything was starting over?" Sure enough, the next morning the husband, wife, and young son awake to discover themselves sole proprietors of the Earth. The story covers only a few crucial hours of time, climaxing in the inevitable moment when the husband makes his second wish:

> Wouldn't it be nice if we went to sleep tonight and in the night, somehow, it all came back. All the foolishness, all the noise, all the hate, all the terrible things, all the nightmares, all the wicked people and stupid children, all the mess, all the smallness, all the confusion, all the hope, all the need, all the love. Wouldn't it be nice.

We sense, of course, that this second wish is not going to come true. So does the couple. As the story goes on, the little details of life, the preparations the couple make for their lifelong picnic, become increasingly irritating to them, serving as reminders of their loneliness. It is interesting to compare the ways in which domestic trivialities make life almost unbearable for this couple with their whole future ahead of them, and the ways in which similar trivialities in "The Last Night of the World" are a source of comfort for a couple with no future at all.

These last two stories bring the world to an end in rather fanciful ways. In the next two stories, the atomic holocaust predicted in "The Garbage Collector" actually takes place. Both stories maintain the intimate, family-centered viewpoint of the stories covered so far; one views the cataclysm from a rather detached location, the other brings us right into the very heart of it.

"The Highway" takes place in Mexico. Hernando, a poor farmer who lives in a thatched hut is disturbed by the mysterious emptiness of the highway that runs by his farm, a highway usually crowded with the automobiles of American tourists. Suddenly the highway is crowded with cars, thousands of them, all rushing north toward the border. Then, just as suddenly, the road is deserted again. "It had been like a funeral cortege. But a wild one, racing, hair out, screaming to some ceremony ever northward." From the occupants of a last car that stops at the farm for some water, Hernando learns that "It's come, the atom war, the end of the world!" This story, like its viewpoint, is only indirectly about the end of the world. It is also a story about endurance and the way different people view their reality. For after the car has left, Hernando goes back to his chores, and he asks his wife the wry and pointed question: "What do they mean, 'the world'?" It is worth noticing that since America is presumably involved in the atom war her citizens are fleeing *toward* the holocaust rather than away from it. Bradbury seems to regard this as a normal reaction, and the situation is repeated in *The Martian Chronicles* when, upon hearing that atomic war has broken out on Earth, virtually all of the colonists on Mars return to the home planet.

We are taken to the heart of the holocaust in "Embroidery." The characteristic elements are present again: a quiet domestic scene, a small number of intimate people, the performance of routine, everyday activities. On a shady front porch, in a rural area, three women work on their embroidery as the warm afternoon wanes. At five o'clock something terrible is going to happen. The exact nature of the disaster is not clear, it seems to be some kind of atomic test: "It's twice as big as ever before. No, ten times, maybe a thousand." Whatever it is, the women know it probably spells disaster and they are not capable of stopping it: "Why didn't we stop them before it got this far and this big?" The women are not only preoccupied with the details of their lives, they also identify the loss of their world in terms of these details.

> The first woman . . . looked through the open porch door, through the warm interior of the quiet house, to the silent kitchen. There upon the table, seeming more like symbols of domesticity than anything she had ever seen in her life, lay the mound of fresh-washed peas in their neat, resilient jackets, waiting for her fingers to bring them into the world.

Another woman is embroidering a landscape scene in which there is a man walking. She suddenly becomes dissatisfied with her work and rips out a number of stitches, removing the man from the scene. At the conclusion of the story, the woman herself seems an embroidered figure in the larger world as the great fire overtakes her:

> The fire caught upon the moving point of the needle while it still flashed; she watched the fire come along her fingers and body, untwisting the yarn of her being so painstakingly that she could see it in all its devilish beauty, yanking out the pattern from the material at hand.

Bradbury portrays the tragedy of atomic war on the level of the individual and the family. In these stories he never considers the political situation. Who is at war or why is unimportant from Bradbury's humanistic standpoint. At the same time Bradbury seems highly fatalistic. His characters see no hope, no chance of reversing the course of events. It is as if once the battle of Armageddon has started the nonparticipants might just as well resign themselves to their inevitable fate. The women on the porch in "Embroidery," the Indians in "Perhaps We Are Going Away," and the townsfolk in "Yes, We'll Gather at the River," all accept the loss of their world without a struggle. In this they echo the behavior of the couple in "The Last Night of the World" who literally lie down and die. But this is not truly fatalism. Bradbury recognizes that the ultimate point of a person's life or world becomes the focal point of all their values. He suggests that the only response to death by those who value living is to go on living, simply, until the last moment. "The Garbage Collector" attempts to take some action to avoid the fate of an atomic war, but his choice is obviously escapist and futile. In any case, the garbage collector's story takes place at a time when something might still be done to prevent the holocaust. In the other stories, in which the disaster has become inevitable, the characters seem to join the rest of the human race in a collective sigh of relief that the anxieties, at least, are over. They would, perhaps, empathize with the husband and wife in "The Last Night of the World" as they turn back the covers on their bed and comment:

> "I'm tired."
> "We're *all* tired."

Bradbury seems to regard man's survival in the atomic age as pretty much of an all-or-nothing proposition. He devotes little attention to the day after the end of the world. "The Vacation" mentioned above is an exception—though, of course, in that story the end of the world is the result of a wish, not a war. Another exception is "The Smile." In a setting reminiscent of that in Shirley Jackson's "The Lottery," a group of townfolk gather to engage in a primitive celebration. Jackson's story is set in an indeterminate time, but Bradbury's is set in a world still in the aftershock of atomic war. As in Jackson's story, the festivity the townspeople indulge in is one of destruction. But Bradbury's characters do not practice human sacrifice, they seek instead to ritually obliterate all remnants of the previous "civilization," which they blame for the shambles the world has become. On this particular day, the people have chosen to destroy DaVinci's *Mona Lisa*. This destruction of works of imagination as a means of cleansing mankind of dangerous passions is a theme underlying several of Bradbury's stories, among them *Fahrenheit 451*, "Pillar of Fire," "The Exiles," and "Usher II," from *The Martian Chronicles*. In each of these stories, the main character endeavors in his own way to preserve what his fellows would destroy. In "The Smile," Bradbury's protagonist, a young boy named Tom, cannot save the whole painting but is at least able to retrieve the fragment of canvas containing the famous smile. The little piece of canvas becomes, in effect, another of Bradbury's magic objects. It is a symbol, for the boy and for us, of art itself, and for its value in human society. But it also generates nostalgia for the past and recreates for Tom some of the emotions generated by the whole painting. It serves as talisman and fetish, linking Tom with the past he never knew, and with the future he must live in. The scrap of canvas has changed Tom; the story implies that he will work to create a new "civilized" world, utilizing the better things the past has to offer.

machineries of joy and sorrow

Rockets • Time Machines • Robots

Man vs. Machine • Orwellian Tales

Fahrenheit 451

Science fiction evolved from the industrial revolution that spawned notions of rockets, robots, time machines, computers, satellites, matter-transporters, and the like. Bradbury's focus nearly always remains upon the human element in his stories, but hardware is a basic element in science fiction and machines inevitably play an important role in his tales about the future.

Rockets

■ If space travel has mythic significance for Bradbury, then rockets represent the tools, the vehicles for the fulfillment of that myth. They are also wonder-inspiring objects themselves. The root of Bradbury's fascination with rockets lies not in the future, but in the past, with remembrances of Fourth of July fireworks:

Fire exploded over summer night lawns. You saw sparkling face of uncles and aunts. Skyrockets fell up in the brown shining eyes of cousins on the porch, and the cold charred sticks thumped down in dry meadows far away.

We never learn much about the mechanics of Bradbury's rockets, for him they seem to be simply crystallized imagination. In "R is for Rocket," fifteen-year-old Chris sees a rocket for what it is, the fulfillment of ages of imagination and myth:

It was a hundred years of dreaming all sorted out and chosen and put together to make the hardest, prettiest, swiftest dream of all. Every line was fire solidified and made perfect, it was flame frozen, and ice waiting to thaw there in the middle of a concrete prairie, ready to wake with a roar, jump high and knock its silly fine great head against the Milky Way.

When Bradbury does give any details about the interior workings of his rocketships, they tend to reinforce the image of a solidified dream. When Fiorello Bodoni steps into the rocket mock-up he notes: "The rocket smelled of time and distance. It was like walking into a clock. It was finished with Swiss delicacy. One might wear it on one's watch fob."

The space ship *Copa de Oro* is specially designed to sweep close enough to the sun to scoop up a piece of it. Outside the ship the sun was so hot it "burned all time and eternity away." Jules Verne might tell us in concrete detail how a ship could perform such a feat, but Bradbury does not. Instead, he portrays the ship as defying the ultimate in summery heat with a mechanically-produced season of its own:

Through corridors of ice and milk-frost, ammoniated winter and storming snowflakes blew. Any spark from that vast hearth burning out there beyond the callous hull of this ship, any small firebreath that might seep through would find winter, slumbering here like all the coldest hours of February.

Besides ignoring the mechanics of rocketry, Bradbury pays no attention to the problems surrounding real rockets. The questions of space appropriations, air pollution, or the perversion of the technology into weapons systems are rarely, if ever, raised. To write a story about man's future among the stars requires some means of getting man to the stars in the first place. Rockets not only make possible the wonders of space travel and man's immortality, they also function as symbols for these wonders and as talismans of good fortune. Bradbury would have us stand with the couple in "The End of the Beginning" as they waited in the darkness and saw ". . . the brightening color in the sky and, ten seconds later, the great uprising comet burn the air, put out the stars and rush away in fire flight . . ." Or with Chris in "R is for Rocket" when ". . . the Dream woke up and gave a yell and jumped into the sky." Like planes and sailing ships before them, Bradbury's rockets are objects of myth and romance. The details of how they operated or where the money came from are ultimately less important than who they carried and where they went.

Time Machines

Modern science has tended to reject the possibility of time travel and so there are few theories about what a time machine would look like and how it would function. Even the classic device in H. G. Wells' *The Time Machine* is only vaguely described. Bradbury's stories about time travel tend to stress the psychological implications or the paradoxes involved, and so place little stress on machinery. Many writers have avoided the use of a machine at all, and have suggested some sort of "warp" or "fold" in the fabric of time to explain travel through this dimension. Though Bradbury does not say so explicitly in the story, some such warp seems to have taken place in "The Dragon." Actually, it is suggested that the moor on which the two knights wait is somehow immune to time. One of the knights says: "On this moor is no Time, is only Forever. I feel if I ran back on the road the town would be gone, the people yet unborn . . ."

Most of Bradbury's stories about time travel do involve a machine of some sort, though it is mentioned only in passing. Time Safari, Inc. operates a commercial time machine in "A Sound of Thunder." Eckels gets an impression of the machine just before he steps into it which is just that— impressionistic.

> Eckels glanced across the vast office at a mass and tangle, a snaking and humming of wires and steel boxes, at an aurora that flickered now orange, now silver, now blue. There was a sound like a gigantic bonfire burning all of Time, all the years and all the parchment calendars, all the hours piled high and set aflame.

This machine has a sort of accessory, a metallic antigravity path which travellers into the past walk on. The path floats above the ground and prevents the time travellers from accidentally touching any part of the world it has not been cleared to touch. As Eckels finds out, such an inadvertent contact might alter the course of evolution. These mechanical items are necessary in "A Sound of Thunder" first, to supply the means of transportation one assumes would be necessary for a safari, and secondly, to explain which paradoxes of time travel will be relevant to the story and which will not. The path, for instance, serves to isolate the incident wherein Eckels alters the future, and allows us to trace just how his misstep had its effect.

No such requirements are necessary in "Forever and the Earth," so we never glimpse the machine which transports Tom Wolfe from his deathbed into the future. Henry Field, who is responsible for the whole plan, simply says to the professor who is perfecting a time machine: "Here's a check, a blank check, fill it in." Even Wolfe has only the vaguest impressions of his trip: "I smelled electricity, I flew up and over, and I saw a brass city. I thought, I've arrived. This is the city of heaven . . ."

Another man who wishes to meddle with the fate of a dead writer builds "The Kilimanjaro Device." This is apparently a modified Land Rover: "I've seen those before . . . a truck like

that in a movie. Don't they hunt rhino from a truck like that?"
Since the story is essentially a fantasy, no further details are
really needed, and none are given.

When Roger and Ann Kristen wish to escape the horrors of
2155 A.D., they take advantage of another professional service, Travel in Time, Inc., to flee into 1938. A government
search party pursues them, armed with a time machine dis-
guised as a motion picture camera. Here again the time
machine is required merely as a prop, so little attention is given
to it. Stories such as these mentioned so far are science fiction
at its most abstract. They seem closest to Bradbury's concept of
the "idea" story, since they derive much of their interest from
the novelty of their premise. These are the most improbable of
the "What if . . .?" stories. "What if we could go back in time?" is
a little like asking "What if two plus two equalled five?" The
trappings of science add a touch of verisimilitude to what, after
all, could only be accomplished by magic. A fine heavy
machine serves as a kind of anchor, stabilizing some rather
flighty speculation, and freeing us to enjoy the puzzles and
paradoxes of an impossible situation. But there is another kind
of time travel, one that is real enough. This is the journey
through memory, a journey we may all take through our own
past, and one we may share with others. For Bradbury, this is a
special kind of time travel, combining as it does reality and
imagination in an intriguingly ambiguous way. If time travel is
viewed as a function of memory, then a human being can be a
time machine. This is indeed the case with Colonel Freeleigh in
Dandelion Wine (see Chapter 6). Objects that arouse or reinforce the function of memory can also be time machines. In
this respect, the attic in "A Scent of Sarsaparilla" is Bradbury's
most elaborate and finely drawn time machine:

> Consider an attic. Its very atmosphere is Time. It
> deals in other years, the cocoons and chrysalises of
> another age. All the bureau drawers are little coffins
> where a thousand yesterdays lie in state. Oh, the attic's a
> dark, friendly place, full of Time.

This attic, which Mr. Finch visits on cold November afternoons, is a massive and elaborate machine. Its controls are many and complex. Yet, because it works directly through the senses, Bradbury is able to portray exactly how it functions. It is a thing of sound: "The attic . . . creaked every bone and shook down ancient dusts." And silence: "The attic was quiet as a thundercloud before a storm." Of light: "His flashlight caught and flickered [chandelier prisms] alive, the rainbows leapt up to curve the shadows back with colors, with colors like plums and strawberries and Concord grapes, with colors like cut lemons and the sky where the clouds drew off after storming." And scent: "The dust of the attic was incense burning and all of time burning."

Finch knows how to operate this machine because he, after all, is the one who built it. The motivation is there in Finch's desire to escape the winter of age and return to the summer of youth. The seasons are obvious symbols in the story, but the central symbol is a sensual experience, the scent of sarsaparilla wafting in through the attic window to call Finch back to the days of his youth. Finch need only put his time machine into operation to return to that long-ago summer:

> If you touched prisms here, doorknobs there, plucked tassels, chimed crystals, swirled dust, punched trunk hasps and gusted the vox humana of the old hearth bellows until it puffed the soot of a thousand ancient fires into your eyes, if, indeed, you played this instrument, this warm machine of parts, if you fondled all of its bits and pieces, its levers and changers and movers, then, then, *then*!

This attic time machine is not so different from Bradbury's rockets. Both types of machine are crystallizations of human imagination, dreams drawn out of the mind and made solid. Each machine is also a metaphor for the stories in which they are found, stories born in Bradbury's mind and realized on the page. The stories, like the machines, take us on a journey through time, space, or a change of season. As in the tales involving magic, Bradbury's consciousness of his own craft is very close to the surface of these stories.

Robots

Few concepts have captivated the imaginations of science fiction writers and their audience as the robot has. The significance of the robot goes far beyond that of a mere mechanical contrivance. In the world of science fiction, the robot represents the ultimate heart of the scientific conceit, wherein man's knowledge of the universe becomes so great that he is able to play God and create other men. So powerful is this idea, and so laden is it with mythical implications, that science fiction has rarely been able to treat the robot realistically. The term robot comes from the Czech *robota* meaning compulsory labor. The name as applied to mechanical men was first popularized in 1921 through Czech playwright Karl Čapek's expressionistic drama *R. U. R. (Rossum's Universal Robots). R. U. R.* contains many classic elements of the robot story as explored by later writers, including Bradbury. In particular, Rossum's robots look exactly like human beings and can be wired to think rationally, even to feel emotions. This leads to the inevitable problems which arise when man creates man. At one point in the play, Helena Glory is so impressed by the robots' resemblance to human beings, that she cannot quite decide how to refer to them, until the manager of the robot factory corrects her:

> HELENA. I saw the first robots at home. The town council bought them—I mean engaged them for work.
> DOMAIN. Bought them, dear Miss Glory. Robots are bought and sold.

Bradbury has created his own robot factory, Marionettes, Inc., whose customers, like those of Rossum's, tend to come to unhappy ends. Bradbury's robots, like Rossum's, look like human beings. Bradbury's characters often come to grief through allowing the difference between a man and a robot to become blurred. Several stories are less than successful due to a similar fuzziness of distinction on Bradbury's part between man and machine.

"Marionettes, Inc." is a horror story as well as a light-hearted warning against taking robots for granted. Braling achieves the dream of the dominated married man and substitutes a mechanical replica of himself to keep his wife occupied while he enjoys a night out with Smith. Braling confides in Smith that he is planning a vacation in Rio, during which the robot will fill in at home with his unsuspecting wife. Smith is awed by the details of Braling's plan as he peruses some of Marionettes, Inc.'s literature. As the literature points out, ". . . while an act is pending in Congress to legalize Marionettes, Inc., it is still a felony, if caught, to use one." This punitive attitude toward the robots seems directed at their potential for facilitating illicit pleasure rather than at their possible use in fraud. Even the company's motto, "No Strings Attached," seems to bear this out. In any case, Braling comes to a suitable comeuppance at the hands of his mechanical double, while Smith, having succumbed to Braling's temptations, receives an unpleasant shock of his own. (Men named Braling have unfortunate experiences with machines in Bradbury's stories. In "Wake for the Living"—not in any of the major Bradbury collections—one Richard Braling comes to grief while investigating his brother's mechanical coffin.)

The use of human-like robots for mere gratification, whether sexual or otherwise, continues to be frowned upon in "Punishment without Crime." In this story, George Hill attempts to relieve his rage toward his cheating wife by murdering her robot duplicate. Marionettes, Inc. duplicates Hill's wife and her bedroom to perfection. So perfect is the robot, that Hill is at first reminded only of the love he and his wife once shared. Hill tries to talk of other matters, but the robot has been programmed with a specific purpose in mind, and so works to arouse his jealous rage. Hill has, after all, paid for this experience. The parallels between the setting at Marionettes, Inc. and a brothel are not lost on Hill, and he briefly demurs:

> "Come to business, then," she said, coldly. "You want to talk to me about Leonard."
> "Give me time, I'll get to it."
> "Now," she insisted.
> He knew no anger. It had washed out of him at her appearance. He felt childishly dirty.

Hill finally does kill the robot, then is subsequently arrested and tried for murder under the "live robot" law. Hill is condemned to death and, at least at first, he accepts the verdict. He knows that objectively he has done nothing wrong, yet he is overwhelmed with guilt:

> After all, they can't let murder be legal. Even if it's done with machines and telepathy and wax. They'd be hypocrites to let me get away with my crime. For it *was* a crime. I've felt guilty about it ever since. I've felt the need of punishment. Isn't that odd?

These are lightweight stories, still they touch upon issues which Bradbury is constantly bringing up in his work. The robots are not people, yet if they are regarded as real, either mistakenly or deliberately, they can produce reactions that are perfectly genuine. Robots are products of invention, they are walking dreams. Like rockets, time machines and short stories, they are made by human hands. But their relationship to us is ambiguous, they generate as many fantasies as they fulfill. Their ultimate value may depend upon our attitude towards them, and the extent to which they stimulate our imaginations.

Three of Bradbury's robot stories are less than successful. They involve robots created as acts of homage to specific people (George Bernard Shaw, Abraham Lincoln, a family's grandmother). Unfortunately, all three stories confuse the homage due to the original person with that given to the robot. Also, the main characters of all three stories make the same mistakes in their attitudes toward robots as Hill did. They accept robots as genuine surrogates for human beings, and in so doing, have their emotional development arrested or thwarted.

In "G. B. S.—Mark V," Charles Willis spends all of his free time aboard a space ship conversing with a robot replica of George Bernard Shaw. Willis is one of Bradbury's loners, passionately committed to his own fantasy world, mocked and misunderstood by his fellow crewmen. But unlike other Bradbury heroes, Willis does not find an outlet for his fantasies in creative behavior. Instead, Willis becomes increasingly attached to what is, after all, a preprogrammed machine. At one point in the story, Willis exclaims, "Oh . . . How I wish I had been alive when you were alive, sir. How I wish I had *truly* known you." The robot answers, "*This* Shaw is best. . . . All of the mincemeat and none of the tin. The coattails are better than the man. Hang to them and survive." An unintentionally ironic assertion, since Willis is plainly talking to the tin and not the mincemeat. Of course the robot means that he represents the quintessence of Shaw's intelligence and wit, with none of the actual man's mortality. But it is in this disregard for the mortality of the original person that this, and the two stories discussed next, stray from the humanistic viewpoint characteristic of most of Bradbury's work. All of the robots aboard the space ship have been placed there for the diversion of the crewmen during the long voyage. The rest of the crew entertains itself with robot women, ". . . all the happy male bees in their hives with their syrupy wind-up soft-singing nimble-nibbling toys, their bright female puppets." Bradbury implies that Willis' conversing with the Shaw robot is a more worthwhile activity, but the story fails to deal with the fact that it is really the same thing. The activities of Willis and the rest of the crew are essentially masturbatory, their fantasies generated and fulfilled within their own minds with no human communication taking place. The crew, at least, recognize what they're doing for what it is. We sense that when the voyage is over, the rest of the crew will be able to resume normal relationships with women. But we cannot be sure Willis will make a similar adjustment. Willis becomes increasingly self-centered as the story progresses. He would, perhaps, be better off with a book of Shaw's. That would at least develop his imagination. As it is, the robot is better than anything Willis could possibly imagine, so Willis becomes merely a rapt listener, a voyeur. At the story's end, the space ship explodes, flinging the crewmen off into space in all directions. Willis and Shaw drift away together, perhaps to be picked up by a rescue ship, perhaps not. Willis has, by this time, become completely selfish. He demands that the robot entertain him: "*Say* it, Mr. Shaw. . . . Say it again. . . . Please sir. . . . I want some more!"

"Downwind from Gettysburg" is centered upon an intriguing idea. A man named Booth puts a bullet through the head of a mechanical replica of Abraham Lincoln—much like the animated robot of Lincoln found at Disneyland. Booth is captured and held in the theater by security guards while Bayes, apparently the theater manager, questions him as to why he did it. Booth says the robot made him jealous—". . . jealous of anything that works right, anything that's perfect, anything that's beautiful all to itself, anything that lasts I don't care what it is!" The opportunity to examine this response to a man-like machine is there, but the story never takes advantage of it. Instead Bayes berates Booth for being a publicity hound, and declares that Booth will not be able to take advantage of what he has done. "You're a has-been that never was. And you're going to stay that way, spoiled and narcissistic and small and mean and rotten." Bayes' contempt for Booth seems based more on the affection Bayes had for the robot than on outrage at Booth's vandalism. The story also attempts to generate some sympathy for the robot's designer, Phipps. But both Phipps and Bayes have confused their feelings about Lincoln with their feelings for the robot to such an extent that Booth appears to be the healthiest of the three. The lack of clarity as to just what the robot is supposed to mean results in an ambiguous and unfocused conclusion.

"I Sing the Body Electric" is almost a commercial for robots as human substitutes. It is the story of three children whose lives are enriched by the arrival of a mechanical grandmother. Bradbury says he wrote this story to help refute the idea that all machines are bad, and much space in the story is taken up with a rather academic argument on the value of machines. The robot is of obvious enough value in replacing the children's recently deceased mother. She can eject kite-flying threads from her index finger, cook fabulous meals, recite all manner of stories from memory, and even recall on command anything a child has ever said to her, spitting it out neatly typed on a piece of paper hidden inside a freshly-baked fortune cookie. But the relationship of child to machine is one dimensional, and the story reveals, in spite of itself, the essential narcissism behind the robot-as-human fantasy. For instance, the electric grandmother alters the appearance of her face so that she resembles whatever child she is talking to. The children all come to love the robot, but it seems just as likely that a child—or any human being—might come to resent a superhuman, all-attentive, all-remembering, all-forgiving, flattering mirror-image of himself. The robot performs the two main functions of a machine to perfection: it serves and it remembers. But the story implies that these are also the functions of a grandmother.

Real grandmothers, unlike Bradbury's machine, often demand service, expect affection, require consideration and adaption to their frailties. The great failure of the robot, which the story seems to ignore, is that it demands nothing of the children, and hence offers them no escape from selfishness. The children do not learn love—the robot needs nothing so the children can give her nothing. At the story's end, the children, finally grown old, can only become selfish children again, fingering the robot's starting key in the hope she will return to tend to their needs.

Man vs. Machine

Bradbury treats the difficulties and threats man can experience from machines more successfully. Robots are not the only mechanical servants which can go awry, and Bradbury has written stories about an impressive number of others. Man can be harmed by machines that are not there when they are needed. "Almost the End of the World" treats this theme in a comic manner, as the world desperately tries to fill its spare time once TV has been taken away forever. In "A Piece of Wood," a young sergeant invents a machine which will do away with another type of machine, specifically by destroying all metals used in weapons. The sergeant's superior officer is horrified at the threat of impending peace. A threat of another kind, with a more poignant resolution is found in "The Flying Machine." The scene is China in 400 A.D. The Emperor Yuan and his servant encounter a man who has made a wondrous discovery:

> In the sky, laughing so high that you could hardly hear him laugh, was a man; and the man was clothed in bright papers and reeds to make wings and a beautiful yellow tail and he was soaring all about like the largest bird in a universe of birds.

It is a flying machine, discovered ahead of its time and, as the Emperor sadly realizes, too far ahead of its time. The Emperor has what few men in history have had, absolute power to turn back the clock. The story maintains the tone of a fairy tale while detailing the tragic decision Emperor and inventor must face.

One of Bradbury's most famous machines is the children's electronic playroom in "The Veldt." The story is a chilling fable, a kind of exaggerated warning to the sort of parents who might, in an earlier age, have let their children watch too much television. Rather than stunt their imaginations as television might have done, however, the electronic playroom brings the children's fantasies to living, breathing, three-dimensional life. When the parents realize that the kids are spending too much time in the playroom, they threaten to pull the plug. But before they can accomplish this, the children conjure up an African veldt, complete with hungry lions, into which the parents are sent on a brief but fatal safari.

The ultimate solution to the problem of pesky home appliances is to be found in "The Murderer." This comic tale consists mainly of a conversation between a man and his psychiatrist. The man has become fed up with his super-mechanized house:

> It's one of those talking, singing, humming weather-reporting, poetry-reading, novel-reciting, jingling-jangling, rockaby-crooning-when-you-go-to-bed houses. A house that screams opera to you in the shower and teaches you Spanish in your sleep.

So, he buys a gun and begins "murdering" the place:

> I ran to the kitchen, where the stove was just whining, "Turn me *over!*" In the middle of a mechanical omelet I did the stove to death. Oh, how it sizzled and screamed, "I'm shorted!" Then the telephone rang like a spoiled brat. I shoved it down the Insinkerator. I must state here and now I have *nothing* against the Insinkerator; it was an innocent bystander.

The story gives enthusiastic support to anyone who has ever been annoyed by gadgets which cause more inconvenience than they alleviate. The concept of the totally mechanized house is developed at greater length, and in a more somber tone, in the chapter "There Will Come Soft Rains" from *The Martian Chronicles* (see Chapter 7).

The ability of machinery to cause destruction at a distance is explored in "Night Call, Collect." The distance here, of course, is in time and not in space. Barton finds himself alone on Mars, and programs an elaborate series of practical jokes into the planet's automatic telephone system. Fifty years later, the phones ring, and Barton listens to the taunts of his own voice. No longer in control of the situation, he is an old man who has forgotten what he did to the phones. But the phone system is in fine shape, and it efficiently leads Barton to his death. The irony of the machine as faithful servant is absolute.

Bradbury's largest and most dangerous machine is nothing less than an entire city. "The City" has waited for 20,000 years on a lonely planet once devastated by Earthmen. When a spaceship from Earth lands again on the planet, the city is waiting to greet it. Bradbury gradually reveals the operation and purpose of the robot city. We watch as it secretly measures and tests the occupants of the spaceship to determine if these are indeed men from Earth. Then, the city suddenly and shockingly reveals itself as a terrible and complex weapon. Bradbury develops in this story what few writers about other planets have done, a true and vivid sense of "alienness." The city operates on principles utterly remote from human values. It performs an act of revenge, but in a completely abstract way, since the offender parties no longer exist and the recipients of the revenge have long since forgotten the crime.

"The Lost City of Mars" is another mechanical town, one that does not enter into combat with its visitors, but which changes them nonetheless. The city is sought by some tourists on Mars, the guests of a wealthy man who wishes to test his new yacht on a recently filled canal. The Martian name for the city is Dia-Sao, "The City of Doom." When the travelers stumble upon the city hidden under a mountain, their presence causes the great sleeping machine to come to life. The gates to the city swing open, air begins circulating, lights go on. The tourists each go their separate way, and each discovers why the city is called Doom. The problem, apparently not foreseen by its builders, is that the city is too perfect. It is a giant wish-fulfillment device which can make fantasies come true so vividly that it becomes a drug. The city exemplifies everything that is wrong with the robots in "G. B. S.—Mark V" and "I Sing the Body Electric." By stealing a person's dreams, the city in effect steals his soul. Cara Corelli, an aging beauty, discovers a "palace of mirrors."

> As she walked through a maze, the mirrors took away
> a day, and then a week, and then a month and then a
> year and then two years of time from her face.
> It was a palace of splendid and soothing lies . . .

This mirror maze echoes the more realistic maze in "The Dwarf" and the more magical maze in *Something Wicked This Way Comes*. All three mazes reflect the unfulfilled wishes of their visitors, with unfortunate consequences.

Parkhill, who has a natural bent for mechanics, finds himself "staring off down a corridor of machines that ran waiting for a solid mile of garage, shed, hoist, lift, storage bin, oil tank, and strewn shrapnel of tools glittering and ready for his grip; if he started now, he might work his way to the end of the giant's ever-constant garage, accident, collision, and repair works shed in thirty years!"

For those in the party mature enough to recognize the function of their fantasies and to not be completely absorbed by them, the city becomes a liberating experience. Harpwell, an alcoholic poet caught in continuous screaming battles with his wife, finds himself alone in a vast room. "In the middle of this room which was roughly a two-hundred-foot circle stood a device, a machine. In this machine were dials, rheostats and switches, a seat, and a steering wheel." Harpwell finds that the machine is a sort of carnival ride that allows its rider to experience violent death as often as he wishes. First Harpwell goes through a fiery car crash: "He felt himself jerked now this way and that. He was a torch hurtled skyward. His arms and legs danced a crazy rigadoon in midair as he felt his peppermint stick bones snap in brittle and agonizing ecstasies." After he has put himself through countless violent deaths, Harpwell emerges from the room a changed man. When he meets his wife, he tells her: "I won't need you any more, dead Meg, Meggy-Megan. You're free, also, like an awful conscience. Go haunt someone else, girl. Go destroy. I forgive you your sins on me, for I have at last forgiven myself."

Aaronson thinks he sees the city for what it is immediately: "no more and no less than an economy-size juke-box ravening under its idiot breath." Actually, the city is somewhat more than this. It is like a living thing, and it has been programmed for self-preservation. It knows how to lure and hold the men it needs. Those it does not need it distracts or disposes of. The self-destructive are encouraged to act upon themselves. As for the outwardly violent, "the hunter" in the party finds himself in the Museum of Weapons. He chooses a gun and begins searching for the heart of the biggest game around, the city itself. Unwittingly he plays into the city's plans and, once disposed of, allows the city to relax and shut down until the next intrusion.

"The Lost City of Mars" represents Bradbury's ultimate machine. It is the logical extension of the electric grandmother in "I Sing the Body Electric." The problem with it is succinctly stated by Wilder: "Good God . . . the place is Hell. The Martians had enough sense to get out. They saw they had overbuilt themselves. The damn city does everything, which is too much!"

Orwellian Tales

Pessimists about the future of mankind have not always envisioned atomic extermination. An uncomfortable survival under a worldwide totalitarion state has also been suggested as a grim possibility. George Orwell's *1984* represents the hub of such writing, and as such it is the logical antithesis of such

Utopian tales as H. G. Wells' *Things to Come*. Bradbury was never keen on Orwell's view of the future, and that attitude has intensified. Recently he has written:

> Nineteen eighty-four will never arrive. Yes, the year itself will show up but not as a Kremlin in gargoyle or an Orwellian beast. We have for the time being, anyway, knocked Big Brother into the next century. With luck and if we keep our eyes on the ballot box and our chameleon politicos, he may never return.

Nevertheless, Bradbury has written two tales of a specifically Orwellian future, "The Pedestrian," and *Fahrenheit 451*. Like many of the end-of-the-world stories discussed in Chapter 4, these works date from the early 1950s, when fears of atomic war and the Cold War were shifting into high gear.

"The Pedestrian" is one of Bradbury's most famous stories, and is a classic example of the Bradbury style of science fiction. The viewpoint is humanistic, and in this case, antitechnological. The story's only character is a loner, self-exiled from his community, sensitive, and with his own set of values. He is also a writer. It is 2053, and Leonard Mead is the last man in his city who goes for walks. Everyone else stays indoors watching television. Mead is a sensualist who takes particular pleasure in the quiet of the empty streets under the moonlight. He is alive and cannot help noticing as he walks through the deserted streets that ". . . it was not unequal to walking through a graveyard where only the faintest glimmers of firefly light appeared in flickers behind the windows." In such a world, Mead is a suspicious character, and in the course of this particular walk he is stopped and questioned by a police car. There are no men in the car, it is only a robot, so Mead is in the position of defending himself to a machine:

> "Your name?" said the police car in a metallic whisper . . .
> "Leonard Mead," he said.

"Speak up!"

"Leonard Mead!"

"Business or profession?"

"I guess you'd call me a writer."

"No profession," said the police car, as if talking to itself.

Unlike the machines which Bradbury likes, the police car has no imagination behind it, nor can it inspire any. The car picks up Mead as a suspected lunatic not because he is behaving strangely, but because his answers cannot satisfy the logic of the machine. When Mead explains simply what he is doing, the machine nearly short-circuits: "Walking, just walking, walking?" Mead admits that no one has bought any of his writing for some time because everyone is watching television. Unlike other Bradbury misfits such as the dwarf, or the old man in "To the Chicago Abyss," Mead cannot turn professional. His problem is a little like that of Marie in "The Next in Line": he is alone and alive in a city of the dead.

Fahrenheit 451

Fahrenheit 451 is one of only two novels Bradbury has written. The other is *Something Wicked This Way Comes.* (*Dandelion Wine* and *The Martian Chronicles* are often referred to as novels, but they are really collections of separate stories unified by theme and specially written bridge passages.) *Fahrenheit 451* is a short novel, an expansion of a story, "The Fireman," originally published in *Galaxy*. The book is about as far as Bradbury has come in the direction of using science fiction for social criticism. Actually, the premise of the book is rather farfetched—that firemen in some future state no longer fight fires but set them, having become arms of a political program aimed at stamping out all literature. This purging of the written word, particularly of the imaginative sort, is found in other stories, most strikingly in "Pillar of Fire" and "The Exiles." But in these other stories the tone is clearly that of a fantasy. *Fahrenheit 451* is realistic in tone, but keeps such a tight focus on the developing awareness of fireman Guy Montag that we can successfully overlook the improbability of his occupation. In fact, the very improbability of Montag's work allows Bradbury to maintain a certain detachment in the book, so that basic themes such as freedom of speech, the value of imagination, the authority of the state, individualism versus conformity, and so on, can be developed and explored without becoming either too realistic or too allegorical.

In the course of the book, Montag goes through what today might be called consciousness raising. He begins as a loyal fireman, burning what he is told to burn, progresses through a period of doubts and questioning, and ends up rebelling against the system and doing his part to keep man's literary heritage alive. But the bones of the plot do little to convey the feeling of the book. Bradbury's world here seems much closer to the present than the future—not so much in terms of its overall structure as in terms of its more intimate details. Some of the characterizations—Montag's wife, given over to drugs and mindless television; Clarisse, an archetypal hippie or flower child; and the old woman, who defies the firemen by pouring kerosene over her books and her own body before striking a match—might have been drawn from the turbulent political events of the sixties. It is almost necessary to remind oneself that *Fahrenheit 451* was published in 1953.

Many of Bradbury's pet themes are to be found in the novel. Metamorphosis is a major theme of the story, for in the course of it Montag changes from book-burner to living-book. Montag the fireman is intensely aware of the power of fire: "It was a special pleasure to see things eaten, to see things blackened and *changed.*" He himself is changed every time he goes out on a job: "He knew that when he returned to the firehouse, he might wink at himself, a minstrel man, burnt-corked, in the mirror."

Machines are of crucial importance. Overall, the book traces Montag's flight from the dangerous mechanical world of the city to the traditional haven of the country. Montag at first feels comfortable with machines, especially his flame-throwing equipment. The first time Montag meets Clarisse he views the scene in mechanical terms: "The autumn leaves blew over the moonlit pavement in such a way as to make the girl who was moving there seem fixed to a gliding walk, letting the motion of the wind and leaves carry her forward." But many mechanical things are repellent to Montag, particularly the equipment the medical technicians use on his wife after she has taken an overdose of sleeping pills: "They had two machines, really. One of them slid down your stomach like a black cobra down an echoing well looking for all the old water and the old time gathered there."

Montag's particular mechanical enemy is the fire station's Mechanical Hound, more like a huge spider, actually, with its "bits of ruby glass and . . . sensitive capillary hairs in the Nylon-brushed nostrils . . . that quivered gently, gently, its eight legs spidered under it on rubber-padded paws." As Montag becomes more fascinated with books and nearer to betrayal of his duties as a fireman, the hound becomes more suspicious of him. The hound is then symbolic of the relentless, heartless pursuit of the State.

When Montag finally flees the city, he must first cross a mechanical moat, a highway 100 yards across on which the "beetle" cars seem to take pleasure in using pedestrians for target practice. Other machines Montag grows to hate are the radio and television that reduce their audience, Montag's wife, for one, into listless zombies.

But *Fahrenheit 451* is not primarily a work of social criticism. Its antimachine and antiwar elements are there primarily as background for Montag's spiritual development. It is interesting that this development seems to be in the direction of social outcast. Granted that Montag's society has its evils, but at the end of the book we are not so sure that Montag will be completely happy with his new-found friends, the book people. What we are sure of is that Montag has entrenched himself as nay-sayer to a society that has become hostile and destructive toward the past. Montag joins the book people whose task, as Granger puts it, is "remembering." But even as he does so, he promises himself that he will one day follow the refugees from the bombed-out city, seeking, though this is not stated, perhaps his wife, perhaps Clarisse. Most of the book people are like the old man in "To the Chicago Abyss," essentially harmless, using their talents for remembering things to aid their society in whatever way they can. But Montag may perhaps be too rigid an idealist, having rejected his former society with the same vehemence as he once embraced it. Like Spender in *The Martian Chronicles,* Montag has committed murder to maintain his freedom and the integrity of his vision. Unlike Spender, but like many of Bradbury's other outsiders and misfits, Montag has successfully achieved a truce or stalemate with a world hostile to his individuality. At the end of *Fahrenheit 451,* Montag's future can go either way; toward reintegration with a new, less hostile society, or toward a continuing, perpetual alienation.

green town, illinois

Dandelion Wine
Something Wicked This Way Comes

Other Green Town Stories

■ Bradbury patterned mythical Green Town after his own home town. Waukegan, Illinois, rests on a bluff overlooking Lake Michigan about forty miles north of downtown Chicago. Strung out along the shore between Chicago and Waukegan are some of the most affluent suburbs in America. But Waukegan is primarily an industrial town, and the factories which line its perimeter, as well as the naval base at Glenview and the Army base at Fort Sheridan, have somewhat isolated Waukegan from the richer towns to the south. In the 1920s, when Bradbury was growing up, Waukegan was decidedly rural, and its primary link with the outside world was the Chicago and Northwestern Railway. When Bradbury lived there, Waukegan was a stop on the railroad's Milwaukee Division, a main line linking Chicago with Milwaukee to the north, and then Minneapolis and St. Paul to the northwest. It is through the C&NW yards and the little station built in 1924 that most of the arrivals and departures at "Green Town" take place. It has been many years since a circus train stopped at Waukegan, but during Bradbury's boyhood, this was a regular occurrence.

Though Waukegan is on the shore of one of the Great Lakes, the lake itself plays a minor role in the stories about Green Town. The fact is, Waukegan does not have the feel of a lake shore town. It is built on a bluff overlooking the lake, but between the foot of the bluff and the shore itself is a confusion of railroad yards, factories, and commercial shipping docks. There is a small yacht harbor and a modest stretch of beach, but an inconvenient road system and the nearby presence of heavy industry inhibit the full use of these attractions.

The railroad station is perched on the top edge of the bluff, and arriving passengers climb a long flight of steps from the tracks below. A block up the street from the station, toward the business section of town, stands the old library building that is featured prominently in *Something Wicked This Way Comes*. The library itself recently moved to more modern quarters. On the corner of Washington and St. James Streets is the home of Bradbury's grandparents, and next door is Bradbury's own childhood home. These houses have been romanticized and embellished in the Green Town stories so that one tends to imagine stately, Victorian style structures, replete with turret-like cupolas and bristling with wrought-iron lightning rods. This image has been encouraged perhaps by some of Joseph Mugnaini's illustrations—particularly for *The Halloween Tree* and the cover of the early paperback edition of *October Country*. Actually, the homes are modest, unadorned frame buildings which, if they have any romance attached to them at all, are of more interest as touchstones in the career of a famous author than as stages for magic or hauntings.

If the houses are something of a disappointment, the ravine certainly is not. Waukegan lies close to the southern-most limit of the glaciers which covered much of the North American continent during the last ice age. As the glaciers receded, they left behind them a soft, crumbly soil called glacial till—primarily clay and gravel mixed with some sand and boulders. The bluffs on which Waukegan and other towns in the vicinity stand are up to eighty feet high, and streams of water left behind by melting glaciers and subsequent rains have, in draining down to the level of the lake, cut deep ravines in the soft till. The biggest and deepest of the ravines in the Waukegan area is well within walking distance of Bradbury's old home. As Bradbury points out in his introduction to the 1976 paperback edition of *Dandelion Wine,* the ravine today is "deeper, darker, and more mysterious than ever." Contributing to this state of affairs is the fact that careless dumping of garbage into the ravine has, in some areas, given rise to a substantial population of rats.

Certainly many actual locations in Waukegan were used by Bradbury in both *Dandelion Wine* and *Something Wicked This Way Comes.* Bradbury even drew a map showing the areas of Waukegan featured in *Dandelion Wine* that was printed in the June 5, 1972 issue of the Waukegan *News-Sun.* But just as certainly, there is little point in searching through real life Waukegan for the truth behind Green Town. For Green Town represents a distillation of Bradbury's experience, a small stage on which people, places, and happenings—many of which entered Bradbury's life long after he left Waukegan—could be created, explored, compared and juxtaposed in a way that would be impossible in an actual town, or indeed in real life.

Both *Dandelion Wine* and *Something Wicked This Way Comes* are charged with an air of fantasy. It is as if Bradbury had come back to haunt his childhood memories that for many years had been haunting him.

Dandelion Wine is a collection of short stories rather than a novel. Many of its chapters can be read, and in fact were published, separately. The unity in the book comes from Bradbury's use of the same group of characters, and from numerous bridge passages written to join the stories together.

While there is much autobiographical material in *Dandelion Wine,* still Bradbury chose to write the book as a fantasy. This allowed him to telescope time at will, introduce characters and events encountered after he left Waukegan, and, in so doing, suffuse his comments upon his own boyhood and on boyhood in general with a nostaligic intensity not possible in the usual memoir.

Bradbury was twelve years old in 1932, when his family left Waukegan to settle first in Arizona, later in California. *Dandelion Wine* was first published in 1957, and what Bradbury has in effect done is to go back to his home town and fill the last summer he spent there with twenty or more years of memories. This explains, in part, the circular structure of the book. The story begins and ends in Doug Spaulding's bedroom. At the beginning there is a sense of something about to happen, summer 1928 is just starting. At the end, it is not surprising that Doug's thoughts cling to the months just past, for he has, in a way, relived Bradbury's entire life in the course of that summer.

As might be expected, many of Bradbury's favorite themes turn up in *Dandelion Wine*. Of these, magic and machinery are the most common. Magic inhabits almost every page of the book. The first acts performed by Douglas Spaulding are those of conjuring. From the cupola of the attic bedroom in his grandparents' house, Doug "magically" awakens the town. The things he causes to happen are commonplace and routine—the lighting of windows across town, the stirring of his family in the house below—but Douglas thinks of himself as a magician. The entire book may be seen as a conjuring trick too in the last scene, in which, back in the cupola again, Spaulding/Bradbury puts the town to sleep again, and ends the story.

In the course of the book, Douglas is surrounded by magical people. Clara Goodwater and Elmira Brown, two would-be witches, engage in a rather futile battle of magic. Ned Jonas, the town's unusual junkman, saves Doug's life with bottles of magic air. Perhaps most striking of the magic people is Colonel Freeleigh.

Freeleigh is a prime example of how Bradbury transported elements from his later life back to his childhood in Green

Town. Bradbury evolved the character of Colonel Freeleigh from his relationships with a number of older people, in particular the famous art historian Bernard Berenson. Berenson wrote Bradbury a fan letter in 1953 in which he invited Bradbury to visit him in Italy. Bradbury recalls: "I was making $90 a week as a writer—and with two children. Three months later, [John] Huston comes along and offers me [the job of writing the screenplay fôr] 'Moby Dick,' and boom, we're off to Ireland. I wrote to Mr. Berenson and said, 'We're coming down to see you.' And I became his 'son.' It was beautiful, and we corresponded from 1953 until 1959 when he died. But, he was Colonel Freeleigh because in October of '59 when he died, all those memories went with him. And you can't go to the grave and say, 'Oh, what about this? Tell me, Colonel, tell me, Mr. Berenson.' It's too late. You've got to do that while they're alive."

Doug Spaulding echoes these sentiments in the book after Colonel Freeleigh dies:

> Yesterday afternoon, at Colonel Freeleigh's house, a herd of buffalo-bison as big as all Green Town, Illinois, went off the cliff into nothing at all. Yesterday a whole lot of dust settled for good. And I didn't even appreciate it at the time. It's awful, Tom, it's awful! What we going to do without all those soldiers and Generals Lee and Grant and Honest Abe; what we going to do without Ching Ling Soo? I never dreamed so many people could die so fast, Tom. But they did. They sure did!

Douglas is referring, of course, to Freeleigh's talent for conjuring up the past with vivid sensory imagery as when he describes a buffalo stampede he witnessed while travelling out West with Pawnee Bill:

> The dust rose up and for a little while showed me that sea of humps, of dolloping manes, black shaggy waves rising, falling . . . "Shoot!" says Pawnee Bill. "Shoot!" And I cock and aim. "Shoot!" he says. And I stand there

feeling like God's right hand, looking at the great vision
of strength and violence going by, going by, midnight at
noon, like a glinty funeral train all black and long and
sad and forever and you don't fire at a funeral train,
now do you, boys?. . .

Obviously, there is quite a bit of Bradbury himself in the
character of Colonel Freeleigh. By writing the book as a fantasy, Bradbury the conjurer, the magician, the technician is
able to merge his own identity with those of several characters
in the story, particularly Leo Auffmann and Ned Jonas.

Leo Auffmann, the technician, builds "The Happiness
Machine," a cunning contraption which takes a rider on a
multimedia trip through many of the beautiful things in the
world. The story parallels that of Fiorello Bodoni in "The
Rocket," save that Auffmann misjudge's his audience's need,
and so fails.

Ned Jonas, seller of potions and talismans, mixes fantasies
and truths to cure Doug of his melancholy. This character of
itinerant magician finds echoes in the lightning rod salesman
in *Something Wicked This Way Comes,* and in the, once again,
melancholy-curing dustman of "A Medicine for Melancholy."

In addition to the cast of magical people, *Dandelion Wine* is
filled with magical wonders as well. Some of these are obvious,
such as the happiness machine, Jonas' bottles of air, and the
mechanical, fortune-telling Tarot witch. But most are more
subtle. Bradbury blurs the distinction between magic and reality for many objects in *Dandelion Wine.* Things seem indistinct,
ambiguous, as if suspended in amber, their significance a
complex combination of reality, passion in the eyes of Doug
Spaulding, and nostalgia in the eyes of Bradbury. These magical things come in all sizes. Perhaps the most famous are the
tennis shoes Douglas buys at the beginning of summer. For
Doug the shoes have the power to transform him into a sort of
wild creature whose dwelling place is summer, and he has a
deep appreciation of their construction:

Somehow the people who made tennis shoes knew what boys needed and wanted. They put marshmallows and coiled springs in the soles and they wove the rest out of grasses bleached and fired in the wilderness. . . . The people who made the shoes must have watched a lot of winds blow the trees and a lot of rivers going down to the lakes. Whatever it was, it was in the shoes, and it was summer.

On a larger scale, what Bradbury did for the attic in "A Scent of Sarsaparilla" he does for the front porch in *Dandelion Wine*. He explores a piece of architecture and shows us how it is supported by magic. Where the attic was a time machine, the front porch becomes a temple where, as "darkness filled the town like black water," the rituals of summer were performed:

These were rituals that were right and lasting; the lighting of pipes, the pale hands that moved knitting needles in the dimness, the eating of foil-wrapped, chilled Eskimo Pies, the coming and going of all the people. . . . Oh, the luxury of lying in the fern night and the grass night and the night of susurrant, slumbrous voices weaving the dark together. . . . And the voices chanted, drifted, in moonlit clouds of cigarette smoke while the moths, like late appleblossoms come alive, tapped faintly about the far street lights, and the voices moved on into the coming years . . .

Machines play an important part in *Dandelion Wine,* and like the other objects in the book, they are as magical as they are concrete. The happiness machine is a failure, but Colonel Freeleigh, whom the boys refer to as "a time machine" is quite a success. Miss Fern and Miss Roberta drive around town in "THE GREEN MACHINE," an old-fashioned electric auto that "purred with the majesty of cats prowling the noontide."

Perhaps the most memorable machine in the book is the trolley that takes Doug and his friends for a free ride during its last run. Bradbury combined his nostalgia for both the Los

Angeles and the Waukegan streetcars that had been replaced
by buses into one vividly portrayed machine:

> Around a curve of silver track, comes the trolley,
> balanced on four small steel-blue wheels, and it is
> painted the color of tangerines. . . . The numerals on
> the trolley's front and sides are bright as lemons.
> Within, its seats prickle with cool green moss. Some-
> thing like a buggy whip flings up from its roof to brush
> the spider thread high in the passing tree from which it
> takes its juice.

Bradbury deliberately makes the trolley seem more
diminutive than it actually was. To see how he selected the
details needed to convey a special picture, we may compare his
description with an actual Waukegan streetcar in the collection
of the Illinois Railway Museum. Bradbury describes the car
mostly in terms of colors, and this alone creates a sense of
insubstantiality to the trolley. The colors in turn are likened to
small things like oranges and lemons. Even the electricity-
gathering pole is compared to a buggy whip. By portraying the
car as riding upon "four small steel-blue wheels," Bradbury
makes it seem like one of the toy electric trolleys sold by Lionel
in the mid-fifties. The actual streetcars in Waukegan were
operated by the North Shore Line, which ran electric rail
service in a number of towns north of Chicago. The specimen
at the Railway Museum is painted in North Shore Line orange,
a bit darker than tangerine. The seats are indeed a dark green
prickly plush, and much of the metalwork is brass or bronze.
But the actual car is very substantial: fifty-one feet long by
eight feet wide by eleven feet high. It runs on two hefty four-
wheel trucks, weighs some 46,000 pounds, and has a seating
capacity of fifty-six. Bradbury's understanding of how an object can conjure up the past, and even seem to freeze time, is
complete, however, and when confronted with the real trolley,
the viewer will like as not find that Bradbury's vision prevails.
For the trolley as preserved is still a relic of an irrecoverable

past, and to ride upon it today is a kind of artificial experience, not far removed from a carnival ride. Doug Spaulding's view of his trolley seems quite accurate, therefore: "The trolley stood like an enchanted calliope, simmering where the sun fell on it." And the function of the trolley as time machine is obvious to all concerned:

> The trolley groaned and swung around an endless green curve, and all the time in the world held still, as if only the children and Mr. Tridden and his miraculous machine were riding an endless river, away.

Most of the machines which Doug Spaulding loves disappear from his life by the middle of the book. The happiness machine is destroyed, the Green Machine abandoned, the trolley replaced by a bus. All become symbolic to Doug of the passage of time, and of his growing realization that he must someday die. Toward the end of the book, Doug becomes fascinated with the mechanical fortune-telling witch in the town penny arcade. Doug's relationship with the witch is similar to that other Bradbury characters have with mechanical people. The human and mechanical aspects of the witch become confused and ambiguous in Doug's mind. Significantly, when Doug is able to obtain the Tarot Witch for himself, he postpones, perhaps indefinitely, an investigation into the inner workings of the creature: "In a year, two years, when I'm fourteen or fifteen, then's the time to do it. Right now I don't want to know nothing except she's here." Thus, self-consciously, Doug postpones dispelling the witch's magic until his impending adulthood will allow him to examine the trickery without a sense of disappointment.

Much of what Bradbury has to say about death may also be found in *Dandelion Wine*. The raw, primitive horror of it is symbolized physically by the ravine, which runs like a scar through Green Town, and personally in the character of The Lonely One. One night, when Doug has been out late, his

mother and his younger brother Tom walk out to the ravine to
look for him. Tom, aggravated by his brother's absence and his
mother's anxiety, begins a series of somber speculations. At
first his thoughts center on the ravine itself:

> They approached, reached, and paused at the very
> end of civilization.
> The Ravine.
> Here and now, down in that pit of jungled blackness
> were suddenly all the things he would never know or
> understand; all the things without names lived in the
> huddled tree shadow, in the odor of decay.
> He realized he and his mother were alone.
> Her hand *trembled*.

Tom then becomes aware of the universal reality of death:

> There were a million small towns like this all over the
> world. Each as dark, as lonely, each as removed, as full
> of shuddering and wonder. The reedy playing of
> minor-key violins was the small towns' music, with no
> lights, but many shadows. Oh, the vast swelling loneli-
> ness of them. The secret damp ravines of them. Life was
> a horror lived in them at night, when at all sides sanity,
> marriage, children, happiness, were threatened by an
> ogre called Death.

This fear of death, which Doug comes to share, is sharp-
ened by the lurking presence of The Lonely One. Though
referred to several times, The Lonely One makes his actual
appearance only once in the book, in one of Bradbury's finest
horror stories. Like many other characters in the book, The
Lonely One is based on a real person. Bradbury says, "The
Lonely One was part of that time when I was six, seven years
old, and the whole town loved to talk about him because he
scared everybody. He was a cat burglar, actually; he'd just
burgle safes and things. He never raped anyone, but I just
changed that slightly. Nevertheless, he was spooky, he was

mysterious, and what a natural thing to write about." The chapter about The Lonely One is a story complete in itself. It follows many of the principles of structure in suspense and horror stories discussed in Chapter 2. During the early pages of the story, Miss Lavinia and her women friends are strolling into town for a movie. The sole topic of conversation is The Lonely One, a maniac who has strangled a number of women in the area. The sense of impending death is built gradually as the women walk through the summer night. Everything from shadows on the walk to meetings with friends become suspicious as the women become increasingly jumpy, and their fantasies become more macabre. The stage is set so well, that in the final pages, when Lavinia must walk home through the dark ravine all alone, the suspense becomes unbearable. Combining as it does extended suspense and a surprise ending, the chapter is a true *tour de force*. But its individual merits aside, the chapter performs a vital function in the context of the book in that it cuts through the rosy, nostalgic atmosphere like a flash of lightning, revealing the harsh interplay of life and death which lie at the heart of Doug Spaulding's experience of growing up.

In the chapters about the ravine and The Lonely One, Bradbury treats death as the terrifying force explored in such stories as *"El Dia de Muerte"* and "The Next in Line." In other parts of *Dandelion Wine* Bradbury treats death as he has in still other stories. When Great-Grandma decides her life is coming to an end, she accepts it with the transcendental calm of the couple in "The Last Night of the World." Where that couple saw their end as ". . . the closing of a book," for Great-Grandma ". . . it was as if a huge sum in arithmetic were finally drawing to an end." There is a reprise of the old man's sentiments in "A Time of Going Away" as Great-Grandma consoles Tom by telling him: "In the Southern Seas there's a day in each man's life when he knows it's time to shake hands with all his friends and say good-by and sail away . . ." To Doug, Great-Grandma relates her personal view of immortality, a miniature version of

Bradbury's cosmic view wherein man's immortality is insured through future generations among the stars: "No person ever dies that had a family. I'll be around a long time. A thousand years from now a whole township of my offspring will be biting sour apples in gumwood shade." And finally, Grandma reflects the vigorous attitude of the old ladies of "There Was an Old Woman," and "Death and the Maiden," as she tells the family: "I've tasted every victual and danced every dance; now there's one last tart I haven't bit on, one tune I haven't whistled. But I'm not afraid. I'm truly curious. Death won't get a crumb from my mouth I won't keep and savor."

Later in the book, when Douglas is overwhelmed by the realization of his own mortality, the Tarot Witch produces a fortune card imprinted with a 17th Century verse:

Hey nonny no!
Men are fools that wish to die!
Is't not fine to dance and sing
When the bells of death do ring?

This high-spirited response to death echoes those of Old Mam ("Death and the Maiden") and Grandma Loblilly ("The Tombling Day") and finds its culmination in Charles Halloway's defiance of death in the concluding pages of Chapter 44 of *Something Wicked This Way Comes.*

If *Dandelion Wine* does not succeed completely, it is probably because of those very qualities which allow it to succeed at all. In the course of the book we are presented with a series of evocatively drawn scenes from childhood which, as in the book's central metaphor, have been bottled like so much wine and set on a shelf to be sampled whenever we wish. But, like bottles of wine on a shelf, the chapters relate to each other primarily because they happen to have been placed next to each other. What we remember, therefore, is a series of images and vignettes, and not really a novel. Most of the characters in the book are confined to their individual chapters, and this too works against a feeling of unity. At the end, Doug Spaulding is a little older, a little wiser, but not even his development has been strong enough to tie the individual stories together. Much of *Dandelion Wine* is as fine as anything Bradbury has written, and if the book seems perhaps a little less than the sum of its parts it should serve as a reminder that Bradbury is, after all, primarily a short story writer.

Something Wicked This Way Comes takes us on another visit to Green Town, again largely through the experience of young boys. But this time the effect is considerably different. *Something Wicked* is a more detached, less introspective work than *Dandelion Wine*. Bradbury uses all of his talents to their fullest advantage in *Something Wicked*, but in this case they are subordinated to compelling plot. *Something Wicked* is Bradbury's favorite novel—his only other true novel besides *Fahrenheit 451*.

Superficially, the two Green Town novels have few things in common aside from the location of their setting. Both use sensory imagery to maintain a vivid mood. *Something Wicked* contains a definite story, a strong plot, and so is less episodic and fragmentary than *Dandelion Wine*. Both books are associated with a specific season, *Dandelion Wine* with summer, *Something Wicked* with autumn. It is on a deeper level that the two books may be seen to have a significant relationship. For the books represent, as do many of the short stories, different facets of the same basic themes, in this case, most profoundly the themes of magic, imagination and the encounter between life and death. *Something Wicked This Way Comes* may also be seen as a continuation and development of the autobiographical aspects of *Dandelion Wine*, particularly as a metaphor for the imaginative process. In *Dandelion Wine*, Green Town seems suffused with magic, but this is seen as a function of Spaulding's sensitivity and imagination. The magic of the front porch, the streetcar, the Tarot Witch, and so on, seems to be a quality of the objects themselves—but this is clearly due to the way Spaulding sees them. In other words, the pervasive magic of 1928 Green Town exists largely in Doug Spaulding's mind, a reflection of Bradbury's nostalgic, romanticized memories. Only in the ravine and in The Lonely One is the magic externalized, the former a symbol of all that is unknown, the latter a personification of Death. This is why there is virtually no conflict in *Dandelion Wine,* save within Doug's mind. Doug is saturated with the magical elements of Green Town, carried upon them like something caught in a tide. He breathes in life and death like the air from the magic bottles of Ned Jonas.

Something Wicked This Way Comes takes place in the autumn of adolescence. The two main characters, James Nightshade and William Halloway are on the brink of their fourteenth birthdays. A key difference between Doug and Tom Spaulding and Nightshade and Halloway is the onset of puberty. Puberty represents the end of childhood, and the point at which the boys begin to distinguish between the internal magic of their imaginations and the external magic of the forces they cannot completely know or control. This is a point which Bradbury accentuates early in the book when Will and Jim accidentally witness a couple making love. The boys have been climbing a tree and view the sexual scene through a second story window. Will is soon frightened by what he sees and drops to the ground. Jim continues watching as Will begs him to come down. "When Jim looked down at last he saw Will as a stranger below with some silly request to give off living and come down to earth." Thus a gap develops between the boys which is never to be closed. Jim looks ahead, eager to grasp life, Will is reluctant to leave the past. Much of Bradbury's character may be seen in these two positions, the curious visionary of the future, and the nostalgic conjurer of the past. Overseeing and commenting on both boys is the character of Charles Halloway, Will's father. He sees Will as one of those people who ". . . get hit, hurt, cut, bruised, and always wonder why, why does it happen? how can it happen to *them*?" As for Jim, ". . . he knows it happens, he watches for it happening, he sees it start, he sees it finish, he licks the wound he expected, and never asks why:

he *knows.*" Charles himself is a dreamer, a boy who never grew up, very much the man his son will one day be.

These three characters must face the invasion of Green Town by Cooger & Dark's Pandemonium Shadow Show. Into this carnival Bradbury has put a host of the characters and devices which haunt many of his short stories: the marionette maker Fantocinni from "I Sing the Body Electric," the woman in the ice coffin from "Drink Entire: Against the Madness of Crowds," the mirror maze from "The Lost City of Mars," and many others. Master of the show, of course, is Dark—the Illustrated Man himself. Whatever part these characters played elsewhere, in *Something Wicked* they represent some manifestation of evil, particularly death. The carnival represents the mystery of the ravine and the threat of The Lonely One expanded and elaborated into a living group of evils against which the main characters must act.

To a certain extent the conflicts in *Something Wicked* are allegorical. Townspeople are lured by the attractions of sex, vanity, or eternal youth. Those who succumb to the temptations are doomed to live out the consequences in some way, as is Miss Foley who takes a ride on the time-machine carousel and winds up a little girl with a woman's mind—a predicament similar to Willie's in "Hail and Farewell." But beyond this, the carnival is a metaphor for the power our dreams can have over us, especially if these dreams have been thwarted or frustrated. The reason for the frustration may not be clear, may even seem mysterious, and from this comes the apparent magical power that the forces of disappointment and fear seem to possess.

Bradbury has said that in writing about Charles Halloway he was, though perhaps unconsciously at the time, writing about his own father. Be that as it may, there is certainly much of Bradbury himself in the character as well. And there is a lot of Bradbury in the characters of Will, Jim, and Dark. To a certain extent, the novel traces the interrelationships of different facets of Bradbury's creative mind. Magician Dark, the Illustrated Man, captivates and terrorizes Will and Jim, his young audience, while Charles Halloway, the boy grown to manhood, explains the deceptions, subverts the boys' fear. Charles Halloway's solution to the threat of Dark and the carnival is consistent with Bradbury's contrariness: in the face of nihilism, simple vigorous affirmation.

Something Wicked This Way Comes ends not in a plunge into adulthood or a reversion to childhood, but rather in a kind of stasis, similar to that of *Dandelion Wine.* The future, age, death, loss of innocence are, for a time, held off. The boys remain poised on the brink of adulthood, the father on the brink of death. Like many other characters in Bradbury's fiction, these three have grappled with their deepest fears and, if not actually victorious over them have at least achieved a temporary peace.

These weightier matters aside, *Something Wicked* is a thoroughly polished work of entertainment. The book may be read as joyous tribute to Halloween. Halloween is very much Bradbury's personal turf, the heart of the October Country ". . . whose people are autumn people, thinking only autumn thoughts." Bradbury's 4th of Julys are encrusted with nostalgia, but his Halloweens are sharp and visceral, impressionistically drawn, but no less vivid or affecting. Bradbury is to Halloween what Charles Dickens was to Christmas, *Something Wicked* is Bradbury's *A Christmas Carol.* Both books revel in the atmosphere of their respective holidays, transforming the apparently superficial accidents of time of year, weather conditions, locale, odors, costumes, and rituals into the heart of the experience itself.

Other Green Town Stories

Bradbury's tales about Green Town and the Spaulding family are not confined to the two novels. Some of these other stories could very well have been included in *Dandelion Wine,* the same way a number of Bradbury's Mars stories could have been part of *The Chronicles.*

"The Night" is the original version of the chapter in *Dandelion Wine* in which Tom and his mother wait at the edge of the ravine for Doug. "The Night" was written in the second person, and it is interesting to compare its technique and impact with the version in the novel, written in the third person.

"The April Witch" is set in Green Town, and though it involves none of Bradbury's usual Green Town characters, it implies that the strange family of "Homecoming" might be distant neighbors of the Spauldings. Another story set incidentally in Green Town is "Time in Thy Flight." This science fiction story includes a description of the arrival of a circus train very much as such a train must have arrived in Waukegan.

Bradbury portrays Spaulding in adolescence in two stories: "A Story of Love," and "One Timeless Spring." As discussed in Chapter 8, "A Story of Love" was based, according to Bradbury, on an actual incident. In its treatment of a love affair between people whose age difference is a barrier, the story parallels the chapter in *Dandelion Wine* dealing with Bill Forester and Helen Loomis. In any case, "A Story of Love" is about a "Bob" Spaulding. To learn of Doug Spaulding's first love, we must turn to "One Timeless Spring." In this story, commensurate with Spaulding's increased maturity, the ravine is no longer a symbol of death, but expands to symbolize all of life's mysteries. As he receives his first kiss in the ravine's embrace, Doug surrenders to the insoluble mysteries of life, love, and death: "I was laughing and crying all in one, and there was nothing to do about it."

Bradbury's grandmother ran a rooming house and, especially during the Depression, a colorful assortment of characters came and went. "Any Friend of Nicholas Nickleby's is a Friend of Mine," and "The Man Upstairs" are fantasies drawn from some of these transients. As many of Bradbury's stories, these two are parallel in many respects, treating the theme of eccentricity in sinister and lighthearted ways. The perception-altering stained glass window in "The Man Upstairs" reappears later on Mars as "The Strawberry Window."

We get a last look at Doug Spaulding, age 40, when he returns to Green Town to commit "The Utterly Perfect Murder." Like Bradbury himself, Doug returns to his home town to settle old scores, perhaps tidy up the past. But Spaulding encounters, as Bradbury did, the strange magic that time and memory, fantasy and reality combine to produce.

mars

The Martian Chronicles

Other Mars Stories

■ One evening in Los Angeles in 1949, Ray Bradbury confessed to his friend Norman Corwin his disappointment at not being able to sell a collection of science fiction stories, including stories about Mars, called *The Illustrated Man*. Corwin, a radio and film producer, convinced Bradbury that his best course was to take the stories to New York and seek their publication personally. Bradbury was making little money as a writer at that time, and his wife Marguerite was expecting their first child. Still, the couple managed to scrape enough together to purchase a single round trip Greyhound bus ticket. After four days and nights on the bus, Bradbury checked into a $1.00 a night room at a YMCA in New York, and began visiting publishers. At first the results were discouraging, since there was a limited market for short stories. Then one night in Luchow's Restaurant, Walter Bradbury (no relation), an editor at Doubleday, asked if the Martian stories didn't form some kind of pattern that enabled them to be connected into a novel. Later, back in his room, Bradbury worked up an outline for what was to become *The Martian Chronicles*. The next day, Walter Bradbury not only arranged a contract for the novel, he also agreed to publish the remaining science fiction stories, and these were eventually published as *The Illustrated Man*. Since its original publication in 1950, *The Martian Chronicles* has, as of this writing, gone through more than eighty printings.

In his stories about Mars, even those which are not included in *The Chronicles*, Bradbury is consistent. The stories are just as solidly set as those written about Waukegan, Ireland, or Mexico. Of course, unlike these other places, Mars had to be created in effect from thin air. In developing his personal image of what Mars was like, Bradbury drew from both nonfictional and fictional sources. Among the nonfiction sources, the most important are "Mr Lowell . . . and his photographs, and earlier sketches by the Italians of the canals of Mars . . ." Important inspiration from fictional sources came from the writing of Edgar Rice Burroughs and Leigh Brackett.

Of the Italian astronomers, the one who perhaps most influenced the image of Mars as developed by science fiction writers was Giovanni Virginio Schiaparelli. It was Schiaparelli who, in the late 1800s, popularized the term *canali* for the network of fine lines he and other astronomers had observed crisscrossing the planet's surface. Schiaparelli was careful not to suggest that the lines might represent some artificial construction, and in fact *canali* is probably best translated so as to imply a natural channel. Nevertheless, the suggestiveness of the translation "canals" was too great for many people to resist.

The American astronomer Percival Lowell (1855–1916) was deeply impressed by Schiaparelli's drawings and, after observing the Martian canals himself, was convinced that Mars not only supported life, but was home to a race of brilliant engineers. Lowell's studies led him to compose elaborate speculations on Martian geology, climate, and politics. Lowell

saw Mars as an ancient world nearing the end of its evolu-
tionary life:

> The drying up of the planet is certain to proceed until
> its surface can support no life at all. Slowly but surely
> time will snuff it out. When the last ember is thus extin-
> guished, the planet will roll a dead world through space,
> its evolutionary career forever ended.

Lowell believed that faced with the evaporation of their
oceans into space, and with the concentration of most of the
remaining water in the polar ice caps, the Martians undertook
an engineering project so huge "the supposed vast enterprises
of the earth look small beside it." Noting that "the extreme
threads of the world-wide network of canals stand connected
with the dark-blue patches at the edge of one or the other of
the polar caps," Lowell concluded that the function of the
canals was to guide irrigation water to the rest of the planet as
one or the other ice cap melted with the change of season.
Because of its blood-red hue, Mars had been named after the
Roman god of war, and the planet was often associated with its
violent namesake. But for Lowell, the planet-wide canal system
was evidence of a world at peace with itself: "The first thing
that is forced on us in conclusion is the necessarily intelligent
and non-bellicose character of the community which could
thus act as a unit throughout its globe." Lowell was a respected,
if controversial figure, and his theories, as well as the opinions
of those debunking his theories, received wide publicity.

As for the fictional influences on his conception of Mars,
Bradbury lists Edgar Rice Burroughs as ". . . first and fore-
most the vulgarian who took me out under the stars in Illinois and pointed up and said, with John Carter, simply: Go
There. . . . Without Edgar Rice Burroughs, *The Martian Chronicles* would never have been born."

Burroughs wrote a series of eleven books about Mars,
featuring the redoubtable John Carter. Carter, a former

officer in the Confederate Army in the Civil War, is mysteriously teleported to the red planet while hiding in a cave from hostile Indians.

Burroughs' Mars is a place of fantasy, with no apologies made. The planet is populated with a bizarre collection of monsters and creatures that resemble human beings, save that they reproduce by laying eggs. Carter goes from one fierce battle to another, pausing occasionally for romantic interludes with scantily clad maidens. Even the surface of the planet, which the inhabitants call Barsoom, resembles a wrestling mat, and is furnished with a "soft and soundless moss, which covers practically the entire surface." The tone of the books is a mixture of Western adventure and sword-and-sandal Biblical epic. The various Martian races are continually at war with one another, and "no male or female Martian is ever voluntarily without a weapon of destruction." The weapons include swords, clubs, and high-powered rifles capable of firing exploding radium projectiles three hundred miles. Martian languages are not very well developed, since most of the population can communicate telephathically. There is a classical touch to Burroughs' Martians too, in that when it is time for them to die, "they go voluntarily upon their last strange pilgrimage down the river Iss, which leads no living Martian knows whither and from whose bosom no Martian has ever returned."

Physically, Burroughs' Mars is similar in many respects to the planet as envisioned by Lowell. The planet is an ancient one, long past its prime. Its seas have evaporated, and the canals are used to circulate water. Burroughs even has the Martians manufacturing their own atmosphere in a special factory. In general, the Burroughs books about Mars are straightforward adventure yarns with an obvious appeal for younger readers. All eleven are still in print, and they continue to be popular in their current paperback editions.

Leigh Brackett, a friend and associate of Bradbury during his early years as a writer in Los Angeles, wrote a number of her own Mars stories. These were obviously influenced by Edgar Rice Burroughs, but boast a refined mythological background and touches of magic and sorcery reminiscent of the writings of the fantasist A. Merritt. Physically, Brackett's Mars is again an ancient planet, crisscrossed with canals and dotted with ruined and half-ruined cities such as "Old Jekkara, with its docks of stone and marble still standing in the dry and dust-choked harbor . . ."

Whatever may be owed to the influences outlined above, Bradbury's Mars is uniquely his own. Like Burroughs and Brackett, Bradbury was not attempting to portray Mars as it actually exists or could exist. But Bradbury was not seeking to write simple adventure stories either. From the start of his project in 1944, Bradbury envisioned an important book about Mars, one which touched upon the deeper human feelings and aspirations. As for the planet itself, Bradbury has never been concerned about the possibility that science would someday prove that there was no life on Mars, or that the planet was quite different from its fictional counterpart. As with Burroughs and Brackett before him, Bradbury's Mars is a mythological place, though in Bradbury's case more classically Greek in atmosphere. *The Martian Chronicles* thus have a certain timelessness about them which even the recent photographs taken from the surface of Mars have failed to dispel. As Bradbury has noted, no one today cares that the Mt. Olympus and the gods of classical Greece never existed. Our encounter with the real mountain does not destroy the power of the myths.

Physically, Bradbury's Mars is a mixture of Lowell's theories and Greek myths. There is a Martian desert which ". . . lay broiling like a prehistoric mud pot," there is a "fossil sea," and canals which "glittered from horizon to horizon." Scattered across the planet are fragile-sounding "ancient bone-chess cities," which contain marble amphitheaters and torch-lit alleyways. In the mountains above the towns are delicate villas with courtyards and fountains. There are roads, but

no signs of heavy industry, and only passing references to
agriculture.

As with *Dandelion Wine, The Martian Chronicles* is not a novel,
but a collection of short stories adapted and linked together by
bridge passages. In many cases, the stories which form the
Chronicles are more varied in tone and less suited to comple-
ment each other than are the stories of *Dandelion Wine*. Indeed,
some seem quite out of place, being horror tales or fantasies
which digress considerably from the main thrust of the book.
The *Chronicles* also lacks the unifying effect of a continuous
group of characters. A few characters pop up repeatedly
through the book, but never to the extent that the book seems
to be about them. But it is this very disjointed, episodic structure that gives the book its overall sense of unity, for the
Chronicles is more than the sum of its parts. The variety of the
stories reinforces the feeling that this is indeed a collection of
chronicles covering the colonization of a planet. It is something
like an elaborate scrapbook in which fact has been bound cheek
by jowl with fiction, to give a multifaceted picture of man's
relationship with Mars. The book may be roughly divided into
three major sections.

The first section deals mostly with the Martians as they
prepare for, or deal with, the invasion of Earthmen, and includes the chapters "Rocket Summer" through "The Third
Expedition." The three main stories in this section typify the
abrupt changes in style and tone which occur throughout the
book. "Ylla" is the only real glimpse we get into the daily lives of
the Martians before the Earthmen arrive. Mr. and Mrs. K live
in a house with crystal walls and fluted pillars. Everything
about the house is impressionistically drawn, presenting us
with a series of contrasting images. Bradbury combines visual
impressions, soft-focused and vague, with tactile images that
are sharp and evocative. For instance, we are told that the
house turns and follows the sun like a flower, and that the
walls are hung with "blue phosphorus portraits"—visual
images which tantalize rather than define. On the other hand,

the description of the house's cooling system is quite concrete: "A gentle rain sprang from the fluted pillar tops, cooling the scorched air, falling gently on her. On hot days it was like walking in a creek." The cumulative effect of the two kinds of imagery is to produce a mixed impression of both house and occupants which is part real, part dream. Bradbury has us stand with Mrs. K in a house as fragile as a tulip in a garden, while our feet are chilled by water streaming across the floor. This delicate combination of fantasy and reality is one of the major triumphs of Bradbury's Mars.

"Ylla" is also the only look we get at some of the intriguing Martian lifeforms which seem to vanish as the book progresses. The house itself almost seems alive, and there are tantalizing glimpses of flame birds and caged flowers. Martian technology is also hinted at in the lava cooking table, the singing books, and the carpet of fog upon which the Martians sleep. There is even a glimpse into Martian history and "tales of when the sea was red steam on the shore and ancient men had carried clouds of metal insects and electric spiders into battle." And we witness a brief trip on a spectacular mode of transportation, a canopy drawn by mysterious flame birds which flew like "... ten thousand firebrands down the wind." Throughout there are touches reminiscent of classical mythology—golden fruits, fluted pillars, wine trees. The story is tied together by the recognizable domestic quarrel which develops between Mr. and Mrs. K. Again, this is our only real look at the interaction of Martians, and their reactions seem surprisingly human.

Bradbury gives us little physical description of his Martians, though brown skin and gold-coin eyes are characteristic traits. Many of the Martians wear masks, which underlines their mystery and the level at which they function as symbols of human dreams about Mars. The ephemeral nature of the Martians and their works contrasts with the more realistically portrayed Earthmen. This functions not only in terms of the plot, but on a deeper level as well. Bradbury was always aware that man might one day reach Mars. Men have dreamt about Mars and other planets for centuries, and science is at last allowing us to confront Mars as it actually is. But scientific data will never be all there is to the Martian experience. The dreams, expectations, and hopes of humankind will go to Mars with every rocket, and our dreams and the scientific information from Mars will interact and color one another. In a way, *The Martian Chronicles* is an extended metaphor for this interaction, and through it, Bradbury is expressing his view of the ways in which dreams and reality coexist in our lives.

"The Summer Night" reinforces the classical Greek atmosphere of Mars, and expands the disturbing telepathic visions which troubled Mrs. K. The tranquillity of the Martian lifestyle, and the unrest the telepathically received thoughts of the Earthmen cause, create a sense of impending doom similar to that faced by the Indians in "Perhaps We Are Going Away."

"The Earth Men" marks quite a jump in tone, a throwback to pulp science fiction. On that level, the story is entertaining, with its satiric view of Martian life, and suggestion that Mars might have its share of what on Earth are UFO fanatics. The conclusion mixes black humor with a touch of the reality-as-function-of-point-of-view theme.

"The Third Expedition" is another improbable tale, but an effective horror story. Mars here provides the sort of fantastic background which allows Bradbury to pull out all the stops and play with themes such as fantasy, nostalgia, magic, illusion, and horror to his heart's content. As is common in such tales, parallels to Bradbury's own art are very close to the surface. In this case, the Martians do to the Earthmen what Bradbury does to us in *Dandelion Wine* and *Something Wicked This Way Comes,* they conjure up an archetypal small town through various sensory images.

"Ylla," "The Summer Night," "The Earth Men," and "The Third Expedition" form a sort of prologue to the *Chronicles.* Their function is not so much to advance the story—which they barely do at all—as to permit Bradbury to recapitulate some of the ways Mars has been treated in fiction: realistically, as fantasy, as pure science fiction, and as the stuff of dreams. The two sections that take place on Earth—"Rocket Summer" and "The Taxpayer"—serve as reference points to which we can return from the more farfetched fantasies. Thus, in this beginning section, Bradbury gets the invasion of Mars off to a good start while avoiding the triteness of a prolonged departure scene. He reminds us of some of the ways Mars has been written about in the past, and tells us that, in the book to come, fact and fantasy will be juggled and juxtaposed.

"—And the Moon Be Still As Bright" begins the main body of the book with an abrupt change in situation. The Martians, who through jealousy or accident or fear destroyed the first expeditions from Earth, have suddenly disappeared. Bradbury again avoids the triteness of an interplanetary war by having the Martians all but exterminated by chicken pox before the chapter begins. This is intriguingly sad, because Bradbury has kept the Martians at arm's length all this time, we've never really had a close look at them, and now, of course, we never will. This chapter introduces the only characters who appear elsewhere in the book, Captain Wilder, Hathaway, and Sam Parkhill. Spender only appears this once, but as one of Bradbury's outsiders, we have seen his like before in William Lantry of "Pillar of Fire," and Montag of *Fahrenheit 451*. It is Spender who does the preliminary research on the Martians, now already the history of a vanished race. Spender discovers a village built of marble with "great friezes of beautiful animals, white-limbed cat things and yellow-limbed sun symbols and statues of bull-like creatures and statues of men and women and huge fine-featured dogs." This suggests that the Martians practiced a sort of Greek pantheism, an idea which Spender finds appealing. We might recall at this point the character George Smith in the story "In a Season of Calm Weather" who encounters Picasso on a beach and watches as the artist draws pictures in the sand: "There on the flat shore were pictures of Grecian lions and Mediterranean goats and maidens with flesh of sand like powdered gold." In any case, Spender finds himself won over to the Martian way of thinking, becoming the first Earthman to turn Martian in the course of the book. But it is Wilder who notes that Martians were ". . . a graceful, beautiful, and philosophical people. They accepted what came to them." If this is true, then Bradbury has given us a hint of what the final days may have been like for the Martians in "The Last Night of the World"—though that story, of course, refers to the last day of Earth. In any case, Spender the idealist, Parkhill the opportunist, and Wilder the pragmatist represent three types likely to be involved in colonization, and their conflict in this early chapter clears the way for the all-out invasion of Earthmen which follows.

The rest of the main section of the book portrays, through vignettes and stories, the settlement of Mars, recalling in many instances the settling of America's West. The stories are, again, a mixture of the plausible and the fantastic. "Way in the Middle of the Air" and "Usher II" do not seem to belong in the context of the other stories, but they function to break up what might otherwise be a pioneer epic and remind us of the social and fantastical elements underlying the book.

The final section of the book begins with "The Luggage Store." Again, the change is abrupt. The colonization seems barely to have gotten started when war breaks out on Earth and most of the colonists return home. Brief attention is given to the fate of those few remaining on Mars, and to the fate of Earth. The book ends with the judgment that humanity's life on Earth represented "a way of life [that] proved itself wrong and strangled itself with its own hands," and with the small consolation that comes from a modest second chance.

Of the themes which run throughout Bradbury's work, the most prominent to appear in *The Martian Chronicles* is that of metamorphosis. Most of the Martians have the ability to change their form to reflect what the Earthmen want to see. In "The Third Expedition" they do this deliberately, but in other chapters, particularly "The Martian," they can be "caught" by a strong Earthman's fantasy and held until a stronger influence comes along or until they can run away. In these cases, the Martians become particularly appropriate metaphors for our dreams. Bradbury seems quite aware that our dreams about Mars are invariably colored by our hopes, and that the reality we eventually confront there will be influenced by both. The Martians' ability to change their appearance is something of a survival mechanism, and it is of course ironic that at the end of the book it is the Earthmen who change into Martians. Thus Mars gives man the chance to change places with his dream, if only in a sad and unexpected way.

Machines play a modest role in most of the book. The machines brought by Earthmen are quite ordinary. The Martian machines reflect a different attitude toward technology, and most are objects of beauty as well as function. Thus the beautiful insect-like walking machine of the Martian in "Night Meeting" contrasts with Gomez's truck. As with the Martians themselves, most of the Martian machines seem spun from fact and fantasy. Most impressive of them are probably the blue-sailed sand ships described in "The Off Season." Toward the end of the *Chronicles*, however, the machines of men assume a crucial importance. In the back-to-back chapters "The Long Years" and "There Will Come Soft Rains," robots become tragic symbols for man's dreams and hopes gone awry. These stories are probably Bradbury's most successful efforts at making the connection between man's imagination and his machines. In "The Long Years" a man makes robot duplicates of his dead wife and children, robots that continue to live on as a family long after the man himself has died. In "There Will Come Soft Rains" we return for a chilling look at Earth after the atomic war, and witness an automatic house brilliantly yet ignorantly continuing to serve a family long dead. "There Will Come Soft Rains" is Bradbury's favorite story, and both stories are certainly among his most moving. They are effective not only because of the skillfully overlapped ironies, but because they touch upon some of the bewildering craziness of humanity which Bradbury takes a special joy in probing.

Bradbury sees much of man's history as continuing cycles of building, then destroying to build again. It is a pattern we do not seem to be able to break, and those who willingly leave or cannot continue the cycle do not survive. Such is the fate of the Indians of "Perhaps We Are Going Away," and of, say, the ancient Greeks whom the Martians may be seen to reflect. Bradbury's Martians have the good taste to take most of their art and science with them when they die. But Bradbury sees modern man so committed to technology, so given to translating his dreams into machinery, that we may wind up having our dreams survive even if we do not. Recently Bradbury has said: ". . . the dream of mankind has been to someday kill death . . . We . . . cry out to the Reaper: Beware of our rocket, which will shatter your scythe and scatter its bits to the stars." *The Martian Chronicles* expresses, perhaps, the cautious hope that if and when these rockets do reach the stars, they will be piloted by something other than computers.

A number of Bradbury's stories about Mars are not included in the *Chronicles,* though in terms of style and consistency with the stories in the book, they could very well be. In fact, two tales, "The Fire Balloons" and "The Wilderness," not included in the current paperback *Chronicles,* were added to the 1973 hardbound edition. "The One Who Waits" could have been included in the opening section dealing with the first ill-fated expeditions. "The Visitor," which tells of a telepathic young man exiled to Mars is an interesting story, but the main character's power would have weakened the idea of the telepathic capacity of the Martians. "The Strawberry Window" should certainly be read in conjunction with the *Chronicles,* especially as part of the middle section dealing with the lives of the pioneers. "The Exiles," which could be substituted for the chapter "Usher II," finds the spirits of Edgar Allan Poe and other writers seeking refuge on Mars from a sterilized Earth. The story, with its thematic tie-in with "Pillar of Fire" is more obviously a fantasy than "Usher II" but has a more touching, less heavy-handed conclusion than the chapter. "The Messiah" and "The Fire Balloons" both describe encounters between Martians and Catholic priests. The latter story involves a species of Martians not otherwise mentioned by Bradbury, while "The Messiah" has obvious parallels to the chapter "The Martian." "The Other Foot" is a sequel to "Way in the Middle of the Air," though in its implication that blacks are the only Earthmen who settle Mars, it does not fit in with the context of the *Chronicles*. "The Lost City of Mars" and "The Blue Bottle" deal directly with Bradbury's concept of Mars as the repository of man's dreams. Both stories concern groups of people searching for an answer in their lives which the city and the bottle come to symbolize. The power given these objects by the cunning of their creators and by the emotional needs of the searchers reflects, of course, the Bradbury brand of magic. As a result, the successful searchers in both stories encounter not only what they seek, but also, and consistent with the quality of their dreams, what they deserve. "Night Call, Collect" would fit in with the stories of the few men left behind when most Earthpeople return to their war torn home. The story has some interesting parallels with the chapter "The Silent Towns," particularly in the use of the telephones to motivate the main character. In both cases Bradbury has fun with the ambiguous relationships between technology and imagination. The phones in "The Silent Towns" set the main character off in pursuit of a dream girl who turns out to be a very different dream than he had in mind. The phones in "Night Call, Collect" send the main character fleeing from himself and from the frightening results of his warped imagination. Finally, the story "Dark They Were, and Golden-Eyed" is almost an alternate last chapter for the novel, and might be substituted for "The Million-Year Picnic." Both tales involve the metamorphosis of Earthmen into Martians. "Dark They Were, and Golden-Eyed" is the more extended and poetic story, and involves a literal transformation. "The Million-Year Picnic" is more suitable in the context of the book because of the tragic irony in the family's having to become Martians as a matter of survival.

other themes

Love and the Circle of Time
Mexico · Ireland · Homosexuals
Religion · Blacks · China

■ Some of the less common themes in Bradbury's fiction are, however, no less interesting. Some of these appear in just one or two stories, and others appear and interact with other elements throughout Bradbury's fiction.

Love and The Circle of Time

Romantic love appears in various manifestations in Bradbury's fiction. It may be as straightforwardly as in "The Great Fire" in which an Aunt and Uncle attempt to cope with the whirlwind love life of their visiting niece. Or it may be combined with elements of fantasy as in the title story from *A Medicine for Melancholy* in which a wandering dustman bestows it upon a young girl as the "Sovereign Remedy" for her chronic *Weltschmerz*. Love represents a strange mixture of remedy and poison to Doug Spaulding in "One Timeless Spring," as Doug, having resisted the attempts of various adults to "poison" him into growing up and leaving his childhood behind, succumbs to the charms of Clarisse whose sweet kiss seals his fate forever. Cecy, the telepathic sister of Timothy in "Homecoming," satisfies her curiosity about love in a special way in "The April Witch." Cecy sends her mind out and possesses the body of a girl named Ann. The story has definite echoes of "The One Who Waits," and Ann is no more willing to be possessed by Cecy than the rocket crewmen are to be possessed by the vapor creature. Cecy forces Ann into going on a date with Tom, and faces a constant struggle trying to build the relationship:

> "Will you miss me?" [asks Tom.]
> "Yes," said Ann and Cecy.
> "May I kiss you good-by, then?"
> "Yes," said Cecy before anyone else could speak.

Cecy has to work hard to experience love, and as other Bradbury characters must struggle to win or hold their heart's desire, the stories become increasingly intriguing. "The Illustrated Woman" consults her doctor about her fear that her husband will no longer find her attractive once he has finished tattooing her body. The doctor finds this a somewhat bizarre relationship, but as it turns out, the worst is yet to come. The striking of strange bargains between couples is carried further in "Some Live Like Lazarus," in which a young man promises to marry his sweetheart as soon as his mother dies. Fifty years later, the sweetheart is still waiting. In "Some Live like Lazarus," the lovers grow old together, but in Bradbury's most interesting love stories the lovers must overcome a great gap in time.

Characters caught in a time in which they do not belong turn up regularly in Bradbury's stories. Two prominent examples from Chapter 3 are the sea serpent from "The Fog Horn" and the boy Willie from "Hail and Farewell." The monster, lacking understanding, was doomed, but Willie, it will be recalled, periodically adjusted his situation by inserting himself into a time frame in which he, temporarily at least, could function successfully. For Willie this was a matter of personal survival. But many of Bradbury's characters must perform similar feats in order to fulfill their love—romantic or otherwise. In *Dandelion Wine*, young Bill Forester, a reporter for the town newspaper, meets ninety-five year old Miss Helen Loomis. The two begin a relationship which culminates, to their mutual surprise, in their falling in love with each other. The sad impossibility of their situation becomes acute as Miss Loomis' death approaches. The lovers must place their hopes in reincarnation which, with a little effort on their parts, might bring them together again in a more fulfilling way. With this in mind, Miss Loomis admonishes Forester:

> You must promise me not to live to be too old, William. If it is convenient, die before you're fifty. It may take a bit of doing. But . . . there is no telling when another Helen Loomis might be born. It would be dreadful, wouldn't it, if you lived on to be very, very old and some afternoon in 1999 walked down Main Street and saw me standing there, aged twenty-one, and the whole thing out of balance again?

This theme of a character, willingly or not, journeying through a circle in time to rejoin a loved one in a time reference in which they can relate, was developed by Bradbury out of a number of episodes in his own life. Some of these episodes have involved a simple difference in age, others have involved romantic love. Bradbury recalls: "I suppose it happens to everyone. It's the same sort of thing with boys at a certain age loving their coaches or heroes or whatever. In my lifetime the people who have influenced me most are writers, librarians, English teachers, and booksellers. . . . Bernard Berenson was really my second father. . . . And Bertrand Russell, I met him in London 24 years ago. I only spent one evening with him, but my god, it was fantastic. . . . We have a very small list of people we want to meet and know and love, and to be able to look them in the face and say that. . . . That's how I felt about George Bernard Shaw. He died in 1950. . . . I didn't make it to Europe until three years later. It was three years too late. In many ways it's like Bill Forester and the old lady."

In "A Story of Love," Bob Spaulding, age fourteen, falls in love with his teacher Ann Taylor. Bradbury recalls: "It's a true story. Some of the conversations are more fleshed out, but, oh my god! was I in love with her. I'd stay after school every day and wash the board and clap the erasers out the window for her and watch the dust fly. I went away from there when I was fourteen. . . . I returned again when I was 26, and she was dead. I had passed her in time, I was older than she was when she died. That was horrible, to realize she was going to be 24 forever, and here I was, older than she was when I was in love with her."

"A Story of Love" varies from reality in that Miss Taylor finds herself returning Spaulding's affection. Also, Bradbury has provided the story with a happy ending, completing the story of Bill Forester and Helen Loomis, in a sense, by implying that Miss Taylor has successfully completed the circle in time and rejoined Spaulding in the "right" time frame.

Obviously things are not tied up so neatly in real life, and Bradbury has touched upon the more tragic consequences of love lost in time in "The Lake." Here again we have a man returning to his home town and recalling the love of his youth. This time it is a love from childhood: "It was that love that is no more bad than wind and sea and sand lying side by side forever." "The Lake" is a ghost story, the two lovers complete their circle in time, but never contact each other directly, but only through an intermediary object, a fragile sandcastle on the beach. This is one of Bradbury's most vivid evocations of the effects of time, distance, and death upon those left behind to remember.

The interrelationships of youth, age, time, and love are explored in other ways in such stories as "The Tombling Day" and "Death and the Maiden." The ventriloquist in "And So Died Riabouchinska" when faced with the loss of his love, attempts to perpetuate his relationship by investing his affections in his dummy. In "The Wish" a man in effect short circuits time by wishing his father alive again on Christmas Eve, so that the two of them might profess their love. Finally, as a side issue, Doug Spaulding attempts to return through time and space for the cause of hate rather than love in "The Utterly Perfect Murder." Doug's plan to murder the bully who tormented him in Green Town thirty-six years before is thwarted when he discovers how time has done the job for him.

Mexico

Bradbury made only one visit to Mexico, but the trip had a profound effect upon him and many of his stories. "I was with a friend of mine. We travelled 9,000 miles in an old beat-up Ford. This was about eight weeks after World War II was over. We had [problems getting gas] and we had to ride on old, ancient tires which threatened to blow out at any moment. It was a totally new experience, going down through Texas, from Nuevo Laredo to Monterrey, then Tamazunchale, then the Mexican plateau." Circumstance and Bradbury's reaction to the alien surroundings began to generate an increasingly morbid atmosphere. For one thing, Bradbury became sensitive to what seemed to be a large number of funerals: "The funerals of older people were easier to accept. But when you see tiny coffins two feet long, or a few feet long, passing you in the street every day, it is immensely sad. And then I was there at the time of the *Dia de los muertos*—the day of the dead—and spent time out on the island of Janitzio on Lake Patzcuaro. Spent all night there in the graveyard with the people." The macabre tone of the tour culminated in a visit to the town of Guanajuato to see the famous mummies so vividly described in "The Next in Line." For Bradbury, this was the last straw: "I got to the end of the corridor surrounded by 110 mummies on all sides, then I had to turn and go back down this corridor toward the light. I didn't think I could make it. I was just horrified by the whole thing . . . I made it to the end and I got up into the light with my friend and I said, 'Hey, let's get the hell out of town . . . I've got this terrible feeling that some time tonight my heart will stop and that I will wind up down here with the mummies.'" Bradbury's friend agreed and the two packed and checked out of their hotel. "We got in our car—and the car wouldn't start. So, I was trapped in Guanajuato over night. And right across the street from the hotel there were two makers of coffins. And they were working on those coffins til 1 or 2 in the morning. So all I heard was little hammers going, and the little nails, and the coffins being made because tomorrow morning three more people were going to be dead . . . and one of them was going to be me. So I couldn't sleep all night and I finally got up and snuck out of the room and went down to the lobby of the hotel and read copies of the *Reader's Digest* till 5 in the morning."

Such experiences are, as Bradbury says, ". . . The mulch of writing . . . You get home, and you work it all out of your system." The direct result of this process in this case are the stories "The Next in Line," "Interval in Sunlight," "And the Rock Cried Out," "*El Dia de Muerte,*" and "The Lifework of Juan Diaz." The first three stories all concern married couples whose relationships are deteriorating. The tone of terror and anxiety is relentlessly maintained, the couples finding little or no comfort in each other. "The Next in Line" and "Interval in Sunlight" are particularly interesting to compare, since they illustrated many of the ways Bradbury handles a given theme in a variety of ways. Both stories have parallel plots which involve a wife's struggles to cope with a ruined marriage. "The Next in Line" dwells upon the woman's morbid fears, and works toward a specifically horrific conclusion. The mummies, symbols of death and the woman's own fatalistic attitude, provide the story with the overall grisly mood characteristic of Bradbury's best horror fantasies. "Interval in Sunlight" is much more of a straight story which achieves its effect through sharp psychological insight rather than through Halloweenish atmosphere, These two stories provide the reader with a rare opportunity to compare identical themes as treated by the same writer from a fantastic and a realistic point of view.

Bradbury's stories set in Mexico are not all grim, of course. "The Lifework of Juan Diaz" uses the mummy idea in a whimsical way. Mexico as a primitive island in a collapsing modern world is touched upon in "The Highway," and the young time-traveling couple of "The Fox and the Forest" find in Mexico a haven from their war torn time.

During Bradbury's early years as a writer in Los Angeles, his office was in a section of town with a large population of Mexican Americans. Bradbury's Latino neighbors turned up in a number of stories. Most of these are straight stories, even though, as in the case of "The Little Mice" occasionally invested with a bizarre tinge. "I See You Never," one of Bradbury's most frequently anthologized stories, demonstrates Bradbury's skill at evoking sensory images to its full advantage in portraying the plight of an illegal alien. As the police take Mr. Ramirez from Mrs. O'Brian's rooming house, Ramirez notices the dining room table ". . . laid with clean white linen and set with a platter, cool, shining glasses, a water pitcher with ice cubes floating inside it, a bowl of fresh potato salad and one of bananas and oranges, cubed and sugared." Mrs. O'Brian, on the other hand, remembers her visit to the border towns Ramirez is being sent back to "—the hot days, the endless crickets leaping and falling or lying dead and brittle like the small cigars in the shop windows . . ."

Two of Bradbury's stories about Mexican Americans resemble some of his Irish stories with their cast of high-spirited characters whose strong sense of camaraderie and an outlandish resourcefulness help them in coping with their problems. The classic tale of this type is, of course, "The Wonderful Ice Cream Suit." But *"En La Noche,"* in which the inhabitants of an apartment building elect one of their number to provide sexual services to a woman whose husband has been drafted, thereby stopping her incessant wailing, should not be forgotten. A third story with something of this feel to it is "Sun and Shadow," which could have been set in Mexico, though Bradbury suggests elsewhere that the location is Puerto Rico. In any case, the story, in which Ricardo disrupts a team of fashion photographers trying to use his crumbling house as a picturesque background, was written as a protest to just such an exploitive fashion layout, which Bradbury happened to see in a magazine.

Ireland

In 1953, John Huston invited Bradbury to Ireland to write the screenplay for the film version of *Moby Dick*. The six months the writer spent in Ireland not only resulted in the screenplay, but also in a number of stories and plays. Most of Bradbury's Irish stories are humorous in tone and take advantage, if sometimes a bit too much, of Bradbury's delight with dialect. Such stories as "The Terrible Conflagration Up at the Place," "The Great Collision of Monday Last," "The First Night of Lent," and "The Anthem Sprinters" are enthusiastic and affectionate—if a bit superficial—appreciations of Irish character. "The Beggar on O'Connel Bridge" is much more serious in tone and, like some of the best of the Mexican stories, starkly outlines the discomfort of middle class Americans in an alien, poverty-burdened culture. "The Beggar on O'Connel Bridge" concerns a Dublin street musician, a subject which Bradbury treats again, though in a lighter vein in "Getting Through Sunday Somehow." Most of the Irish stories are "straight"—involving no fantasy or science fiction elements—and most seem closely related to Bradbury's actual experiences in Ireland. (Most of the stories are told from the viewpoint of a visiting American, in particular, a writer.) The exception is "The Haunting of the New" an updated ghost story.

Homosexuals

Two of Bradbury's Irish stories involve homosexuals, and others involve encounters with unconventional sexual life-styles. While living in Ireland, Bradbury was struck by how similar some of his new Irish friends were, in their drinking in pubs, with some of his homosexual friends back home. Bradbury acknowledges that had he mentioned this to any of his Irish friends, their response might have run something like, "My God! Put your hat on, will you, so I can knock it down!" Nevertheless, Bradbury resolved to write a humorous story involving the Irish and some homosexuals—humorous because he felt that most stories involving homosexuality ". . . take themselves too seriously. They've all got to end unhappily, and . . . that's not the way life is." The result was "The Cold Wind and the Warm," in which the denizens of a Dublin pub encounter a group of visiting American homosexuals and are astonished to find they have much in common.

In "The Better Part of Wisdom," an Irish grandfather who knows he is dying and who is making a last trip to say goodby to his relatives, discovers that his grandson is living with a male lover. To the grandson's surprise, the grandfather is understanding, recalling a friendship he himself had with another boy when he was twelve. The recollection hooks the reader into understanding something about the grandson as well, Bradbury believes. "We all have love affairs when we are children that are never equalled in our late days . . . where you walk through the world transfigured by your friendship . . . the love of being alive in the universe. You walk around, you look at clouds, you lie on hills, you hold hands, but you don't even know why you are holding hands—except this is your best pal." Both "The Cold Wind and the Warm" and "The Better Part of Wisdom" seem to take the right approach in touching the reader's understanding, but both also depend upon their key figures—the men in the pub and the grandfather—behaving in what must strike most readers as rather unlikely ways.

Bradbury lures our sympathy for unorthodox sexual behavior quite subtly in "Long After Midnight," by arousing our
feelings for one thing and then substituting another. Unfortunately, the story conceals its heart until the very end. Bradbury
does give us some unsympathetic homosexuals too in the
flamboyant crowd involved in the kidnapping of "The Parrot
Who Met Papa."

Religion

Bradbury has considerable difficulty in treating religious
themes successfully in his fiction. Many stories dealing with
Christianity sentimentally attempt to reconcile that religion
with the implications of space travel or life on other worlds.
Since, at least at the present time, the space travel and the
lifeforms are speculative to begin with, the speculations about
their effect on Christianity seem academic at best. "The Man"
is about what happens to the crew of a rocket that lands on a
planet, apparently just after Christ has been there. The story
dwells on the conflict between the simple faith of the believers
and the relentless skepticism of the rocket's captain. The story
never really moves beyond the stereotypes.

Four stories involve Catholic priests. All, except for the
"straight" tale "Have I Got a Chocolate Bar for You!" involve
the impact of space travel upon religion. "The Machineries of
Joy" is little more than an academic discussion between an Irish
and an Italian priest about the religious implications of space
flight. "The Fire Balloons" and "The Messiah" are about encounters between Catholic priests and Martians. "The Messiah" is a story that parallels the chapter "The Martian" in *The
Martian Chronicles*. Both episodes involve earthmen who meet
Martians with the power to alter their appearance to whatever
shape the Earthmen imagine. The priest sees the Martian as
the image of Christ, and doesn't want to let him go. "The Fire
Balloons" contains some interesting material on interspecies
communication as some Catholic priests attempt to convert

Martians who appear as glowing blue spheres. But more interesting is a shift by one of the priests toward transcendentalism: "The way I see it there's a Truth on every planet. All parts of the Big Truth. On a certain day they'll all fit together like the pieces of a jigsaw."

Transcendentalism of a sort is the theme of Bradbury's quite successful religious story, "Powerhouse." Here, a woman who has been unable to find solace in any organized religion, undergoes a mystical experience while spending the night in a remote electrical power station. Bradbury's descriptive powers carry the story:

> The earth was suddenly more than many separate things, more than houses, rocks, concrete roads, a horse here or there, a human in a shallow, boulder-topped grave, a prickling of cactus, a town invested with its own light surrounded by night, a million apart things. Suddenly it all had one pattern encompassed and held by the pulsing electric web.

Bradbury's nonfiction essay "Zen and the Art of Writing" may be considered an interesting adjunct to the transcendental aspects of this story. Bradbury's advice to the writer in his essay is basically to relax and let the creative energy flow: "The time will come when your characters will write your stories for you, when your emotions . . . will blast the page and tell the truth." The woman in "Powerhouse" realizes her unity with the universe by relaxing and letting the humming energy of the electricity flow through her: "Whether it was with understanding, acceptance, joy, resignation, she couldn't know. The singing went on, higher and higher, and she was everywhere."

"Powerhouse" also contains Bradbury's most extended essay on electricity. For Bradbury's many machines, electricity is life itself. Not only does it give the gadgetry movement and light, but in so doing it provides an accent, almost like a sharp spice, to the stories. A typical example is the Green Town trolley: "From every window blows an incense, the all-pervasive blue and secret smell of summer storms and lightning."

Blacks

It is somewhat startling to come across a story like "The Big Black and White Game" in a collection of fantasy and science fiction stories such as *The Golden Apples of the Sun*. Bradbury's stories are rarely political, though they may occasionally be inspired by some political situation. "Pillar of Fire," for instance, "was caused by the quasi-intellectuals who mob through our society bullying us about our tastes, telling us that comic-strip cartoon books are bad for our digestion, worse for our imagination, and so should be burned. I would gladly Gunpowder Plot these ignorant social reformers out of existence, at least in my stories . . ." As typified by "Pillar of Fire," Bradbury's stories usually express his views indirectly, in this case allegorically. But there is nothing indirect about "The Big Black and White Game." It is a straightforward, unblinking view of racial prejudice. The plot involves a baseball game between the white guests of a Wisconsin resort hotel and the hotel's black servants. The story is told from the point of view of a twelve-year-old white boy who is watching the game with his mother. From the beginning the atmosphere is tense, and it is clear that racial supremacy is an issue in the game: " 'Look at them prance,' said Mother. 'You'd think they thought they were going to win the game from our men.' " Bradbury's ear for dialogue is precise and merciless, and the white spectators reveal the depth of their prejudice with every line they speak. This is not without touches of humor. When the blacks, who are first at bat, promptly drive in seven runs, Douglas' mother comments, "They're the most inconsiderate people." But the story is not an inflammatory tract on race relations. The tone itself is almost journalistic—in fact, the description of the game itself is a fine piece of sports writing—and the point, when finally made, is a quiet one. Because of the disturbance at the game, none of the white people show up that night at the big dance in the pavilion. Only the black people are there. Young Douglas sneaks over to the pavilion and watches the dancing, aware, it seems, that his mother and her friends have, through their own blindness, denied themselves some of the simple pleasures of life: "It was so dark all around the pavilion; the stars shone in the black sky, and I stood outside, my nose against the window, looking in for a long, long time, silently." The situation of the story is obviously dated, and Bradbury's approach seems occasionally quaint. But the story is largely a period piece, and what is surprising about it, apart from being in a collection of fantasy, is that it was first published in 1945.

Bradbury's ear for dialect again serves him well in the chapter "Way in the Middle of the Air" from *The Martian Chronicles*. This traces what happens in a small southern town when the entire black population departs in a rocket for Mars, and has a much more contemporary feel to it. Ironically, in the context of the book the chapter now seems a little old-fashioned, the scenario somewhat unlikely for the year 2003.

"The Other Foot" is a kind of sequel to "Way in the Middle of the Air" and is based on the premise that blacks are the *only* people who migrate to Mars. The story deals with the arrival of a spaceship piloted by white men—some of the few survivors of an atomic war on Earth. As the title implies, this is a tables-turned sort of story, fairly common in science fiction, in which characters suffer complete role reversals. In this case, the blacks must decide how they will treat the whites whom they now vastly outnumber. Unlike the other stories, this one ends on a note of hopeful optimism—an optimism readers will balance against their own opinion of human nature.

China

Bradbury's two stories about China have themselves something of the feel of oriental fairy tales. This is particularly true of "The Golden Kite, The Silver Wind," in which the Mandarins of rival cities engage in a charmingly symbolic arms race. Using the tactics reminiscent of the children's game stone-paper-scissors, the Mandarins alter the outline of their cities' walls so as to put the other city at a disadvantage. The walls of one town are built in the shape of a pig, an animal capable of devouring the city whose walls are shaped like an orange. Bradbury's writing here is full of whimsy as in the reaction of one city's stonemasons to the news of what their rivals in the other city have been up to:

> Here the stonemasons groaned and wept. Death rattled his cane in the outer courtyard. Poverty made a sound like a wet cough in the shadows of the room.

Fortunately, one of the Mandarins has a wise daughter and, thanks to her efforts, the fable ends with a proper moral, espousing a sort of intercity *detente.*

"The Flying Machine" is more serious in tone. Bradbury says that he ran across a supposedly factual historical note regarding a Mandarin of the 12th or 13th century who discovered a man flying with bamboo wings. The Mandarin had the man beheaded and burned with his machine. "Well, I was so taken with that that I sat right down and, three hours later, I had my short story." Bradbury likes the theme of the story because it points up intriguing questions about the values and dangers of technology and about how questions about progress are decided. For instance, with respect to the development of atomic energy, ". . . you say, that's all bad, isn't it?. . . Then you stop and think . . . how about its being all good? Or how about its being halfway good? Because since [the development of the atomic bomb] we've had no major wars. Little ones—Korea, the Middle East and Viet Nam. But we haven't killed forty million people a year . . . it's not the big holocaust of the other wars. So, the atom bomb and the hydrogen bomb have preached Christianity to us . . . That's a hard paradox to accept, because we want things in clear terms . . . and they never are . . . they never will be."

other work

Film · Plays
Children's Books · Poetry

■ The work considered in this chapter lies outside the general limits imposed upon this study. Nonetheless, it is of interest in terms of its relationship to themes discussed so far, and in contributing to an overview of Bradbury the writer.

Film

A self-styled "child of motion pictures" from the age of three, Bradbury lost little time, once he had established himself as a professional writer in Los Angeles, in getting acquainted with members of the film community. He arranged to meet John Huston, a particular hero of his, in 1951, at which time he presented the director with copies of *The Martian Chronicles* and *The Illustrated Man.* Huston was duly impressed, and later wrote Bradbury from Africa, where he was working on "The African Queen," promising that the two would one day work together. Finally, as mentioned before, Huston invited Bradbury to his home in Ireland to work on the screenplay for "Moby Dick." For Bradbury, the task was educational and laborious. The final screenplay ran about one hundred thirty pages, but this had been painstakingly boiled down from an original treatment more than ten times that length. Though the film had its moments, it was not an overall success. The pacing sometimes dragged, and the film was probably too long. Huston experimented with a new color process intended to tone down the garish hues of many Hollywood films, but this only resulted in a murky feeling to the photography. Bradbury himself was reportedly not pleased with Gregory Peck's performance as Ahab. Though he respected the actor, Bradbury felt that in this case Peck had not brought the proper quality of madness to the role. Overall, the film came off as a ponderous, if respectful, tribute to Melville which never quite developed the energy to live by itself.

More important perhaps from the standpoint of Bradbury's writing was the effect his contact with Melville and Ireland was to have on his fiction. For Bradbury, the character of Ahab came to typify the gesture of maddened rage which is one possible response to the forces of nature and the inevitability of death. In his introduction to the 1962 Bantam paperback edition of *20,000 Leagues Under the Sea*, Bradbury compares Ahab's attitude to that of Jules Verne's mad Captain Nemo. Technology allows Nemo to transcend Ahab's fate. By building his submarine, Nemo "becomes" a whale, and dwells in the very sea which Ahab fears. The essay is one of Bradbury's few theoretical works, and explores, through its comparison of Ahab's fatalism and Nemo's technological optimism, many of the mythical underpinnings of science fiction. As has been mentioned, the attitude of Stubb, with his laughter in the face of whatever the future holds, crystallized some of Bradbury's own sympathies enough to be recalled in the epigraphs to *Something Wicked This Way Comes*.

Bradbury sought to be faithful to Melville in "Moby Dick," so the film reflected few of his own personal themes. The first film to do this to any extent was the 1953 science fiction horror movie "It Came from Outer Space." Bradbury did not actually write the screenplay for this, but only the treatment upon which the screenplay by Harry Essex was based. Nevertheless, the film contains a heavy dose of the Bradbury fascination with metamorphosis. The story concerns an alien space ship which crashlands in the Arizona desert and is concealed in a cave by its occupants while they search for materials to effect repairs. In order to pass unnoticed among the humans in the area, the aliens transform themselves into copies of local persons and animals. The plot thickens when the ship is discovered and the main characters begin to search for the invaders. The aliens are reminiscent of Bradbury's Martians in their talents for changing form and, in spite of their peaceful intentions, for terrifying Earthlings. The creatures also recall Bradbury's amorphous monsters, being shapeless, if in this case corporeal, blobs. The film was cleverly photographed in 3-D, so that effects such as a human arm materializing out of thin air are carried off with a creepy panache. It was a low budget effort, but the acting was competent and the photography and direction good enough so that the film stands as one of the better fifties sf-horror movies. The thrills of 3-D are lost when the picture is shown on TV, but may be seen to full advantage from time to time at science fiction film festivals.

Few of Bradbury's earlier efforts at screen and TV writing are likely to be seen by the general reader. Episodes for TV shows such as "The Alfred Hitchcock Hour" and "The Twilight Zone," as well as the short film version of "Icarus Montgolfier Wright," are rarely shown. As of this writing, Bradbury is said to be working on scripts for a film version of *Something Wicked This Way Comes* and a TV adaptation of Wil Huygen and Rien Poortvliet's book *Gnomes*.

Turning to films written by others but based on stories by Bradbury, the first is the 1953 thriller "The Beast from 20,000 Fathoms." There is little likelihood that a reader of the original *Saturday Evening Post* story—collected under the title "The Fog Horn"—would recognize it as the source of the filmscript.

Bradbury's carefully evoked tone of eerie melancholy was completely abandoned in favor of monster-running-amok-in-the-city cliches. The briefest reference to the lighthouse and its keepers is made before the film settles down to depicting the beast's destructive rampage through New York. This was the first major showcase for the talents of Ray Harryhausen, who followed Willis O'Brien, creator of "King Kong," as Hollywood's major specialist in three-dimensional animation. The movie was, in many respects, a pale imitation of parts of "King Kong," and in it may be seen the seeds of still lesser imitations, such as the "Godzilla" series. The ending of the movie is ironic, though probably unintentionally, in that the monster is finally trapped in the wooden coils of an amusement park roller coaster—the same sort of ride which, lying in ruins on a beach in California, inspired Bradbury to write the story in the first place.

"The Beast from 20,000 Fathoms" provided an ominous foretaste of the sort of treatment Bradbury was to receive from Hollywood. In the films made so far, none has successfully translated Bradbury's poetic and evocative imagery to the screen. Even in later years, when filmmakers attempted to be more faithful to the original stories, the results left much to be desired. François Truffaut's version of *Fahrenheit 451* was a good try which perhaps should not have been made. The main problem here was in translating Bradbury's premise to the screen. As discussed in Chapter 5, Bradbury's stylistic approach to the story allows us to accept the unlikely existence of "firemen" whose job is to set fires rather than fight them. But on the screen, the literal picture of a fire truck and crew driving about the city burning books seems rather absurd. In the novel, Montag's inability to maintain communication with either his wife or the mysterious Clarisse adds depth to his characterization, but in the film, the continuing presence of Julie Christie as the seemingly obligatory Hollywood love interest keeps the story on a mundane level. Still, the film has its moments, and many of its limitations may be ascribed to an insufficient budget. Bradbury himself enjoyed the last scene in which the book people stroll about reciting their memorized passages to themselves, and he believes "Fahrenheit 451" to be the best film adaptation of his work so far.

Jack Smight's film "The Illustrated Man" is even less successful, this in spite of a considerable amount of talent and money expended on the production. The film consists of three stories from the collection of the same name plus a greatly elaborated version of the Illustrated Man encounter used to frame the stories in the book. The three tales dramatized are "The Veldt," "The Long Rain," and "The Last Night of the World." The first two segments stick fairly close to the stories, but this is somehow not enough. A camera shot of the rain-soaked jungles of Venus, for example, lacks the Baroque richness of Bradbury's prose, so the experience seems diminished and trivialized. Bradbury's mood of restrained calm in "The Last Night of the World" is completely shattered by pumped-up dialogue and a weak, melodramatic ending. A sense of unity for what in the book are unrelated stories is attempted by assigning the major roles in all three segments to the same actors. But this creates some confusion in that the viewer is never sure whether or not these are supposed to be the same characters, or whether or not the stories are intended to relate to one another in some unexplained way.

"The Beast from 20,000 Fathoms," "Fahrenheit 451," and "The Illustrated Man" all appear occasionally on television. A fourth film, "Picasso Summer," based loosely on the story "In a Season of Calm Weather," made a brief appearance on television in 1972, and has since all but disappeared. "Picasso Summer" had some interesting moments, including some clever animation based on Picasso's paintings—particularly *Guernica*—yet it lacked the compact development and the poignant conclusion of the original story.

In spite of the disappointing results achieved so far, Bradbury is convinced that his work can be successfully adapted to the screen. One of the main problems to be solved, as he sees it, is the translation of his written metaphors into visual ones. In discussing a hypothetical filming of "A Sound of Thunder," for instance, Bradbury suggests that he would film the dinosaur in such a way as to convey visually what the prose passage suggests: that the beast is an amalgamation of horrors. This would involve moving in close to reveal the chain-mail-like texture of the animal's hide, perhaps showing little parasites scurrying among the scales. Bradbury would then focus on the little front claws to allow the viewer to appreciate their fastidious cunning. A major defect Bradbury sees in the films discussed above is their failure to stick close enough to his original story: "There's nothing wrong with 'The Veldt' that just ripping the pages out and stuffing them in the camera wouldn't cure."

It is difficult to say whether or not Bradbury's views on the filming of his work are correct, what is certain is that no one has, as yet, tried it his way. For the present, at least, the Bradbury experience remains a literary and not a cinematic one.

Plays

Having been an amateur magician in Waukegan, read funnies over the radio in Tucson, and written and performed in theatrical productions in high school in Los Angeles, it was probably inevitable that Bradbury would one day begin converting some of his short stories into plays. It was not until 1964, however, that, encouraged by friends and his own conviction that he was ready, Bradbury finally produced a full-fledged theatrical event called *The World of Ray Bradbury*. This collection of three one-act plays ran for twenty successful weeks in Los Angeles, Bradbury reports, but went on to flop in New York. Though no further productions seem to have been as unsuccessful as the one in New York, most of Bradbury's theatrical efforts so far have just about broken even. Two collections of plays are available in book form: *Pillar of Fire and Other Plays*, which contains dramatic versions of "Kaleidoscope" and "The

Foghorn" in addition to the title story, and *The Wonderful Ice Cream Suit and Other Plays,* which includes "The Veldt" and "To the Chicago Abyss."

In some ways it is less difficult to translate the stories into plays than it is to translate them into films, since drama is largely a verbal medium and doesn't require constant adaptation of Bradbury's written metaphors into visual ones. On the other hand, Bradbury's stories are often mood pieces in which physical descriptions are very important. Within the confines of a comparatively bare stage, however, the mood must be established and maintained almost entirely through dialogue. This cannot be stretched too far, and in fact the focus in the dramatization of a story must inevitably shift from mood and atmosphere to characterization, for it is primarily the actors and their relationships which produce the effect, not the scenery or the situation. In the play version of "The Foghorn," Bradbury's descriptive interludes must be dispensed with entirely, and the dialogue between McDunn and Johnny considerably modified. McDunn's lengthy monologue must be broken up to avoid boring the audience, and Johnny's part must be expanded so that he becomes a character in his own right, and not just the explanation for McDunn's speaking out loud that is his reason for being in the story. The monster itself can hardly be brought on stage, so it must be described by the two men for the audience. Here the dialogue must be compromised with the fact that Bradbury's evocative description of the serpent is not likely to issue from someone's mouth in ordinary conversation. Most of the plays in the volumes above reflect the difficulty of dramatizing stories in which characterization was largely subordinated to an idea or an emotional effect.

"The Wonderful Ice Cream Suit" was a story which depended very heavily on characterization and as it turns out, it has been the one most successfully converted to a play. It has been received enthusiastically by both public and critics in a number of professional productions around the country. Several of Bradbury's Irish stories started out as plays, and it is interesting to note that the Irish stories as a group are perhaps Bradbury's most consistently "dramatic" in terms of character interaction and sprightly dialogue.

Most of Bradbury's plays have been based on his own stories, but one, "Leviathan '99," is based upon his encounter with *Moby Dick.* The play parallels the novel, and deals with a space ship in pursuit of a giant comet. At this writing, Bradbury is reworking the play into an opera.

Although, with the possible exception of "The Wonderful Ice Cream Suit," the quality of Bradbury's plays does not measure up to his fiction, his affection for the form allows us the valuable opportunity to examine his failures as well as his successes in carrying an idea from one medium to another.

Children's Books

Bradbury has written two children's books: *Switch on the Night* and *The Halloween Tree.* William F. Nolan reports in *The Ray Bradbury Companion* that *Switch on the Night* was a story developed by Bradbury to teach his daughter Susan not to be afraid of the dark. Both books, in fact, reflect Bradbury in a parental role dealing with subjects potentially frightening to children. *Switch on the Night* takes the more imaginative approach, and suggests that a child find release from a fear of the dark through a creative act. The story concerns a little boy who, because he fears darkness, stays in the house all evening while his friends play outside. One night while his parents are away, a little girl appears at the door and introduces herself with the words "My name is Dark." The girl shows the boy how to alter his point of view so that the light switch is no longer a device which turns something *off,* namely the light, but rather a magical device which switches on the many wonders of the night. Having conveyed this bit of wisdom, the girl disappears, leaving the boy to join the other children in their nighttime games. Bradbury's themes of magical people and things influencing perception, and reality as altered by point of view is very much in evidence in this book, so: besides teaching children how to get over a fear of the dark, it also provides a quick introduction to Bradbury philosophy.

The Halloween Tree deals with another fearful subject, that of death, but this time the approach is historical. The place is Green Town, Illinois; the time, early evening on Halloween; the cast, a group of young trick-or-treaters who are taken on a trip through time and space to see how various cultures cope with death—the "Undiscovered Country." The tour guide is Moundshroud, obviously Death, and he takes the boys to see funeral rites of ancient cavemen, Egypt at the time of the Pharaohs, Britain during the time of the Druids, Europe during the Dark Ages, and Mexico during *El dia de Muerte*. In the course of the book, we encounter many characters and situations from other Bradbury stories, such as the torch-wielding caveman from "The Golden Apples of the Sun," Death as the Grim Reaper from "The Scythe," the candy skulls from *"El Dia de Muerte,"* and the cavern of mummies from "The Next in Line." The book is thus not only a brief history of man's death rituals, but also a kind of recapitulation of Bradbury's fictional treatment of the conflict between life and death. It comes as no surprise, therefore, when, near the book's end, Moundshroud voices some distinctly Bradburyian sentiments. One of the boys asks, *"O Mr. Moundshroud, will we* EVER *stop being afraid of nights and death?"* To which Moundshroud replies: *"When you reach the stars, boy, yes, and live there forever, all the fears will go, and Death himself will die."* Once again in *The Halloween Tree*, Bradbury is able to bring the streets of Green Town alive during his favorite time of year, and readers of *Something Wicked This Way Comes* will find themselves right at home. Unfortunately, in deference to the young audience at which *Halloween Tree* is aimed, Bradbury strains a bit too hard to maintain an overall jaunty tone. With a lighter touch, the entire book could be as effective as the passage in which the boys must surrender one year of their lives to Moundshroud in order that Pipkin be spared.

Poetry

Though Bradbury's poetry had to wait until relatively late in his career to be widely published, it is actually one of his earliest forms of literary expression. In fact, Bradbury's first appearance in print was the poem "In Memory of Will Rogers," published in the Waukegan *News-Sun* in 1936. Considering the poetic quality of so much of his prose, it is difficult at first to understand why most of Bradbury's poetry doesn't measure up to the quality of his fiction. The images which flow so spontaneously and build so effortlessly in many prose passages often seem contrived and cramped in the restricted line length of the poems. Consider his passage from the story "The Next in Line" dealing with a child's funeral in Mexico:

> It was no ordinary package the first man in the procession carried on his head, balanced delicately as a chicken-plume. It was covered with silver satin and silver fringe and silver rosettes. And he held it gently with one brown hand, the other hand swinging free.

And compare it with this stanza from the poem "Death in Mexico":

> They carried her like jewels overhead;
> The father balanced her, hand up, gently as a plume,
> A crated feather, a valley flower, an April grass,
> And no one wept.

The several similes for the father's balancing gesture and his burden in the poem—plume, crated feather, valley flower, April grass—are not cumulative in their effect, merely repetitive, and together they are not more effective than the single and more appropriately mundane image of the chicken-plume in the prose passage. The line "And no one wept" seems a sentimental interjection in the poem, and in any case, less subtle and less visual than the image of the father's "other hand swinging free" from the story—an image which implies rather than declares the father's lack of anguish. Bradbury also has a tendency to bring together in the same poem subjects so vast and frequently unrelated that even the most epic treatment is insufficient to tie the subjects together, let alone move on to some poetic synthesis. Such is the case in the cantata "Christus Apollo," and the poems "Old Ahab's Friend, and Friend to Noah Speaks His Piece" and "Emily Dickinson, Where Are You? Herman Melville Called Your Name Last Night in His Sleep!"

Other criticisms might be brought up, such as Bradbury's unfortunate affection for the easy rhyme, but there is probably no use harping on them. Bradbury has not exactly forced his poetry on the public, and what he has published is, for the most part, clearly of a personal and often experimental nature. Bradbury is at his best when his macabre sense of humor and his taste for rhymes combine in a children's poem such as "Groon":

> Does it . . . bump . . . 'neath your bed
> Near the head or the toe?
> When it's there, *is* it there?
> When it's gone, where's it go?

Their artistic qualities aside, Bradbury's poems touch upon many themes covered in this book. The poems mentioned above, for instance, deal with such themes as death, Mexico, religion, Herman Melville, and Halloween. Some poems cover ground already treated in various stories. "Some Live Like Lazarus" parallels the late-awakening to life theme of the story of the same name. "I, Tom, and My Electric Gran" is an obvious reworking of "I Sing the Body Electric."

One poem in particular touches the heart of the Bradbury experience. In "Remembrance," the speaker returns to his boyhood home, recognizable to us because of its ravines. The speaker seeks a message left by himself as a child and addressed to the man he would one day be. The message, hidden in a tree, becomes a magical device which allows its seeker to complete a circle in time and to encounter his past self in a new and disquieting way. When the circle is completed, the child caught up in the future and the man lost in the past become so closely linked that it is no longer clear where one ends and the other begins. This is Bradbury's special world, where dreams of tomorrow and memories of yesterday become parts of the same fantasy, and where, therefore, it is quite appropriate for the child to say to the man: "I remember you."

10

looking ahead

■ Many of the stories upon which Ray Bradbury's fame rests, were written and published in relative obscurity, and with little reward other than the joys of the craft itself. As Bradbury's popularity has increased in recent years, his literary output, especially fiction, has dwindled, and for his fans, the occasional appearance of a new story is a special event. Not that Bradbury is inactive. He is in demand as a lecturer, regularly invited to National Aeronautics and Space Administration (NASA) functions, involved in producing his plays, designing entertainments for WED Enterprises, and occupied with a host of other projects.

As for the fiction, it may be that, like the space program, which, in his lifetime, has grown powerful enough to land cameras on Mars itself, Bradbury is only pausing to assess the progress made so far and to choose a path into the future. A novel is promised soon, but when it appears it will probably only increase the demand for still more books and stories. But Bradbury will not be placed in the position of one of his metamorphic Martians, to be pushed and plucked at by anxious fans who would change him into an endless fountain of short fiction. He has followed his own independent lights so far, and shows every evidence of continuing to do so. In discussing his work on the operatic version of "Leviathan '99," Bradbury says: "It's a gorgeous experience. And again, it's a chance to fail—which I think is important—a chance to be a student again. And if that isn't at the back of everything you do in your life, you better give up. . . . Because if you play it safe, what a boring life you're going to have. Just go on writing *The Martian Chronicles* the rest of your life? No, no, no way. Do something really bad. And get kicked a little. And then get up and do it over."

Whatever the quality and quantity of Bradbury's fiction in the future, whatever form his artistry takes, his place as a major figure in the science fiction pantheon is secure.

To a generation of mainstream readers, Bradbury *is* science fiction, with the stories he published in *Collier's, The Saturday Evening Post,* and *Esquire.* To sf fans, Bradbury is almost the grand old man whose work has included practically every science fiction theme, from robots to time travel, from other planets to other realities.

The great magician Blackstone, who handed the boy Bradbury a live rabbit from a hat in Waukegan, Illinois in 1931 knew not what he wrought. Bradbury the man became himself a person of magic, a man who shared his dreams with millions of readers. Every Bradbury fan has a number of memories created by Bradbury's art—the looming jungle from "The Veldt," the frightening mechanical persistence of the automated police car in "The Pedestrian," the air of despair around the empty house in "There Will Come Soft Rains," the graceful spires of the Martian cities in *The Martian Chronicles.*

H. G. Wells said that his own work would hold the reader "by art and illusion"—as good a description of Bradbury's work as any, for his art extends from the realm of science fiction into that of fantasy, creating for the reader the quiet, tree-lined streets of Green Town, Illinois, the mind of a boy, and the dreams of youth.

Few writers have tried to bring to life small-town America in the 1920s and Earth colonies on Mars in the next century, carnivorous dinosaurs and the horrors of a Mexican graveyard, families of friendly vampires and societies reminiscent of George Orwell's *1984*.

It is to Bradbury's credit that not only has he tried to make all these live for his readers—he has succeeded.

Notes

Full bibliographical information is given in the Notes only if the work is not listed in the Bibliography, or if it is necessary to distinguish between different editions of the same work. References to "Interview" apply to an unpublished interview between the author and Ray Bradbury that took place on October 5, 1978 in Los Angeles.

Preface

Page	Quote or Reference	Source
xi	"They are all fantasies . . ."	H. G. Wells, *The Complete Science Fiction Treasury of H. G. Wells,* p. iii
xii	"Every time we try . . ."	Harlan Ellison, ed.,*Again, Dangerous Visions,* pp. 188–189.
xii	"has lifted itself . . ."	Clifton Fadiman, "Prefatory Note," Bradbury's *The Martian Chronicles* (New York: Bantam Books, 1954), p. vii.

Chapter 1

Page	Quote or Reference	Source
1	"My mother took . . ."	Interview.
2	"I was on the radio . . ."	Interview.
2	"Likes to write stories . . ."	William F. Nolan, *The Ray Bradbury Companion*, p. 48.
2	"I sold a story . . ."	Interview.
4	"in my early twenties . . ."	Ray Bradbury, "Just This Side of Byzantium, An Introduction," in Bradbury's *Dandelion Wine* (New York: Bantam Books, 1976), p. vii.
4	"Something like this . . ."	Bradbury, *Zen and the Art of Writing*, p. 13.
4	"The answer to writing . . ."	Interview.
4	"When I was 25 . . ."	Ibid.
6	"Any of us who wish . . ."	Ibid.
6	"A sound of thunder . . ."	Bradbury, "A Sound of Thunder," from *The Golden Apples of the Sun*, p. 94.
7	"I'll make a voice . . ."	Bradbury, "The Fog Horn," from *Golden Apples*, p. 17.
8	"(I hear) a voice . . ."	Bradbury, "The One Who Waits," from *The Machineries of Joy*, p. 17.
8	" 'Sam,' Bittering said . . ."	Bradbury, "Dark They Were, and Golden-eyed," from *A Medicine for Melancholy*, p. 100.
12	"you're nothing but . . ."	Lewis Carroll, *Alice in Wonderland and Through the Looking Glass* (New York: Grosset & Dunlap, 1946), p. 133.

Chapter 2

14	"Coffee . . ."	Bradbury, "To the Chicago Abyss," from *Machineries of Joy*, p. 193.
15	"What did I have . . ."	Ibid., p. 199.
15	"Like this . . ."	Bradbury, "The Visitor," from *The Illustrated Man*, p. 130.
16	"She wanted to touch . . ."	Bradbury, "The Great Wide World Over There" from *Golden Apples*, p. 103.
16	"I walk along . . ."	Bradbury, "The Man in the Rorschach Shirt," from *I Sing the Body Electric*, p. 252.
17	"as if a cork . . ."	Bradbury, "Getting Through Sunday Somehow," from *Long After Midnight*, p. 103.

Page	Quote or Reference	Source
17	"Imagine you're an American . . ."	Ibid., p. 106.
17	"stood like a hollowed . . ."	Bradbury, "The Day it Rained Forever," from *Medicine for Melancholy,* p. 173.
18	"blood moving fast . . ."	Bradbury, "The Drummer Boy of Shiloh," from *Machineries of Joy,* p. 45.
18	"Rubber, steel, clay . . ."	Bradbury, 'Tyrannosaurus Rex," from *Machineries of Joy,* p. 22.
18	"Perhaps . . . perhaps . . ."	Bradbury, "The Rocket," from *Illustrated Man,* p. 185.
19	"that willing suspension . . ."	Samuel Taylor Coleridge, *Biographia Literaria,* chap. XIV. Quoted here from *English Poetry and Prose of the Romantic Movement,* George Benjamin Woods, ed. (Chicago: Scott Foresman and Company, 1950), p. 398.
19	"Inside the walls . . ."	Bradbury, "The Miracles of Jamie," from *After Midnight,* p. 236.
21	"think about that jar . . ."	Bradbury, "The Jar," from *The October Country,* p. 88.
21	"sunny pleasure-dome . . ."	Bradbury (quoting "Kubla Khan" by Coleridge), "A Miracle of Rare Device," from *Machineries of Joy,* p. 121. For the complete test of "Kubla Khan," see *The New Oxford Book of English Verse,* Sir Arthur Quiller-Couch, ed., (New York: Oxford University Press, 1939), pp. 668–670.
21	"Right now, I'm feeling . . ."	Bradbury, "A Miracle of Rare Device," from *Machineries of Joy,* p. 126.
22	"before Garibaldi!"	Bradbury, "The Marriage Mender," from *Medicine for Melancholy,* p. 60.
22	"There was Mars . . ."	Bradbury, "The Strawberry Window," from *Medicine for Melancholy,* pp. 171–172.
24	"Are we not fine . . ."	Bradbury, "The Wonderful Ice Cream Suit," from *Medicine for Melancholy,* p. 31.
25	"Dog had rattled . . ."	Bradbury, "The Emissary," from *October Country,* p. 105.
27	"He gets some . . ."	Bradbury, "The October Game," from *After Midnight,* p. 244.

Page   Quote or Reference   *Source*

28 "The public is . . ."   François Truffaut (quoting Alfred
                                        Hitchcock), *Hitchcock*, p. 52.

29 "She did not think it . . ."   Bradbury, "The Next in Line," from
                                        October Country, p. 18.

29 "You just skit out . . ."   Bradbury, "There Was An Old
                                        Woman," from *October Country*,
                                        p. 225.

30 "the sugar skull . . ."   Bradbury, *"El Dia de Muerte,"* from
                                        Machineries of Joy, p. 92.

31 "I'm young! . . ."   Bradbury, "The Tombling Day,"
                                        from *Body Electric*, p. 199.

31 "I know not all . . ."   Herman Melville, *Moby Dick*, chap.
                                        XXXIX (New York: Grosset &
                                        Dunlap, n.d.), p. 191.

34 "with a gliding ballet . . ."   Bradbury, "A Sound of Thunder,"
                                        from *Golden Apples*, p. 94.

34 Bradbury recalls . . .   Interview.

35 "From the surface . . ."   Bradbury, "The Fog Horn," from
                                        Golden Apples, p. 4.

35 "It comes in the window . . ."   Bradbury, "The Wind," from
                                        October Country, p. 199.

37 "It was as if . . ."   Bradbury, "The Women," from
                                        Body Electric, p. 50.

38 "I live in a well . . ."   Bradbury, "The One Who Waits,"
                                        from *Machineries of Joy*, p. 14.

39 "Did he sleep . . ."   Bradbury, "Homecoming," from
                                        October Country, p. 250.

40 "I live alone . . ."   Bradbury, "Uncle Einar," from
                                        October Country, p. 194.

41 "I tried to stay . . ."   Bradbury, "Hail and Farewell,"
                                        from *Golden Apples*, p. 158.

42 "He scowled . . ."   Bradbury, "The Dwarf," from
                                        October Country, p. 15.

42 "Your baby . . ."   Bradbury, "Tomorrow's Child,"
                                        from *Body Electric*, p. 34.

43 "Those *Geographic* . . ."   Bradbury, "A Time of Going
                                        Away," from *Medicine for Melan-
                                        choly*, p. 127.

45 "I'm dead, I'm dead . . ."   Bradbury, "Jack-in-the-Box," from
                                        October Country, p. 173.

45 "Get going. It's *after* us!"   Bradbury, "The Burning Man,"
                                        from *After Midnight*, p. 41.

46 "There are silences . . ."   Bradbury, "The Smiling People,"
                                        from *The Small Assassin*, p. 133.

46 "Is—is he dead?"   Bradbury, "The Crowd," from
                                        October Country, p. 154.

Page	Quote or Reference	Source

47 "Wouldn't it be fun . . ."   Bradbury, "The Cistern," from *October Country*, p. 239.

48 "when his back . . ."   Bradbury, "The Fruit at the Bottom of the Bowl," from *Golden Apples*, p. 38.

Chapter 4

50 "Learn what . . ."   Bradbury, "The Machineries of Joy," from *Machineries of Joy*, p. 9.

50 "A million years ago . . ."   Bradbury, "The Golden Apples of the Sun," from *Golden Apples*, p. 167.

51 "Icarus Montgolfier Wright . . ."   Bradbury, "Icarus Montgolfier Wright," from *Medicine for Melancholy*, p. 84.

51 "It's really the end . . ."   Bradbury, "The End of the Beginning," from *Medicine for Melancholy*, p. 23.

51 "Is this how it was . . ."   Bradbury, "The Wilderness," from *Golden Apples*, pp. 30–31.

52 "From the opened case . . ."   Bradbury, "The Rocket Man," from *Illustrated Man*, p. 66.

52 "out into space . . ."   Bradbury, "The Gift, from *Medicine for Melancholy*, p. 140.

53 "For a long time . . ."   Bradbury, "The Rocket Man," from *Illustrated Man*, p. 74.

53 "When I'm in Boston . . ."   Bradbury, "No Particular Night or Morning," from *Illustrated Man*, pp. 106–107.

54 "like a dozen . . ."   Bradbury, "Kaleidoscope," from *Illustrated Man*, p. 19.

55 "planet 7 . . ."   Bradbury, "Here There Be Tygers," from *R is for Rocket*, p. 97.

56 "was a mizzle . . ."   Bradbury, "The Long Rain," from *Illustrated Man*, p. 53.

56 "lay . . . outside forever . . ."   Bradbury, "A Scent of Sarsaparilla," from *Medicine for Melancholy*, p. 76.

57 "a great black ship . . ."   Bradbury, "The Fox and the Forest," from *Illustrated Man*, p. 116.

58 "The birds, his hands cried . . ."   Bradbury, "Perhaps We Are Going Away," from *Machineries of Joy*, p. 72.

Page	Quote or Reference	Source
59	"Man survives . . ."	Bradbury, "Almost the End of the World," from *Machineries of Joy*, p. 70.
	"Moore finally touched . . ."	Bradbury, "Yes, We'll Gather at the River," from *Body Electric*, p. 90.
60	"After the atomic bombs . . ."	Bradbury, "The Garbage Collector," from *Golden Apples*, p. 147.
61	"A war?"	Bradbury, "The Last Night of the World," from *Illustrated Man*, p. 91.
	"Wouldn't it be nice . . ."	Bradbury, "The Vacation," from *Machineries of Joy*, p. 36.
63	"It had been . . ."	Bradbury, "The Highway," from *Illustrated Man*, p. 40.
63	"It's twice as big . . ."	Bradbury, "Embroidery," from *Golden Apples*, p. 75.
65	"I'm tired."	Bradbury, "The Last Night of the World," from *Illustrated Man*, p. 93.

Chapter 5

68	"Fire exploded over . . ."	Bradbury, "The Fire Balloons," from *Illustrated Man*, p. 75.
68	"It was a hundred years . . ."	Bradbury, "R is for Rocket," from *R is for Rocket*, p. 3.
68	"The rocket smelled . . ."	Bradbury, "The Rocket," from *Illustrated Man*, p. 181.
68	"burned all time . . ."	Bradbury, "The Golden Apples of the Sun," from *Golden Apples*, p. 165.
69	"the brightening color . . ."	Bradbury, "The End of the Beginning," from *Medicine for Melancholy*, p. 25.
69	"the Dream woke up . . ."	Bradbury, "R is for Rocket," from *R is for Rocket*, p. 4.
69	"On this moor . . ."	Bradbury, "The Dragon," from *Medicine for Melancholy*, p. 8.
70	"Eckels glanced . . ."	Bradbury, "A Sound of Thunder," from *Golden Apples*, p. 89.
70	"Here's a check . . ."	Bradbury, "Forever and the Earth," from *After Midnight*, p. 177.
70	"I've seen those . . ."	Bradbury, "The Kilimanjaro Device," from *Body Electric*, p. 7.
71	"Consider an attic . . ."	Bradbury, "A Scent of Sarsaparilla," from *Medicine for Melancholy*, pp. 74, 75.

Page   Quote or Reference   *Source*

115 "There on the flat shore . . ."   Bradbury, "In a Season of Calm
                                             Weather," from *Medicine for
                                             Melancholy*, p. 4.

116 "a graceful, beautiful . . ."   Bradbury, *The Martian Chronicles*, p.
                                             54.

117 Bradbury sees much of . . .   Interview.
118 "the dream of mankind . . ."   Bradbury et al., *Mars and the Mind of
                                             Man*, p. 137.

122 "Will you miss me . . ."   Bradbury, "The April Witch," from
                                             Golden Apples, p. 20.

123 "You must promise me . . ."   Bradbury, *Dandelion Wine*, p. 152.
123 "I suppose it happens . . ."   Interview.
123 "It's a true story . . ."   Ibid.
123 "It was that love . . ."   Bradbury, "The Lake," from *October
                                             Country*, p. 99.

125–26 Various quotes   Interview.
127 "laid with clean . . ."   Bradbury, "I See You Never," from
                                             Golden Apples, p. 70.

128 the location is Puerto Rico . . .   Bradbury, *Zen and the Art of Writing*,
                                             pp. 29–30.

129 Various quotes   Interview.
131 "The way I see it . . ."   Bradbury, "The Fire Balloons,"
                                             from *Illustrated Man*, p. 90.

131 "The earth was suddenly . . ."   Bradbury, "Powerhouse," from
                                             Golden Apples, p. 117.

131 "The time will come . . ."   Bradbury, *Zen and the Art of Writing*,
                                             p. 22.

131 "Whether it was . . ."   Bradbury, "Powerhouse," from
                                             Golden Apples, p. 118.

131 "From every window . . ."   Bradbury, *Dandelion Wine*, p. 97.
132 "was caused by . . ."   Bradbury, *Pillar of Fire and Other
                                             Plays*, pp. ix–x.

132 "Look at them prance . . ."   Bradbury, "The Big Black and
                                             White Game," from *Golden Ap-
                                             ples*, p. 78.

134 "Here the stonemasons . . ."   Bradbury, "The Golden Kite, The
                                             Silver Wind," from *Golden Apples*,
                                             p. 65.

134 Bradbury says that . . .   Interview.
135 He arranged to meet . . .   Interview.
137 "The Beast From 20,000   Details about the making of this
       Fathoms"   film from Ray Harryhausen's
                                             point of view, as well as informa-
                                             tion on other Harryhausen films
                                             may be found in *From the Land
                                             Beyond Beyond*, by Jeff Rovin.

139–40 Various quotes   Interview.

Page *Quote or Reference*	*Source*
140 This collection . . . New York.	Bradbury, *The Wonderful Ice Cream Suit and Other Plays*, p. vii.
140 Though no further . . . broken even.	Interview.
142 "Leviathan '99" . . . an opera.	Ibid.
143 "O Mr. Moundshroud . . ."	Bradbury, *The Halloween Tree*, p. 143.
144 "It was no ordinary . . ."	Bradbury, "The Next in Line," from *October Country*, p. 17.
144 "They carried her . . ."	Bradbury, "Death in Mexico," from *When Elephants Last in the Dooryard Bloomed*, p. 49.
145 "Does it . . . bump . . ."	Bradbury, "Groon," from *When Elephants*, p. 82.
146 "I remember you."	Bradbury, "Remembrance," from *When Elephants*, p. 6.

Annotated Bibliography

No complete bibliography of Ray Bradbury's work exists at this writing, and since it is beyond the scope of this book to include one, the listing below is confined to sources quoted from or consulted for this book. Until a complete bibliography does appear, those produced by Indick, Nolan, and Slusser (as listed below) may be helpful. Except for the most recent collections, which were widely distributed in hardcover, I worked primarily from the paperback editions of Bradbury's books, since they are the most readily available. The dates shown are, of course, from the specific edition used, but note that in many of the earlier or later paperback editions of the same title—especially among the Bantam editions—the page references remain valid.

Works by Ray Bradbury

"The Ardent Blasphemers." Introduction to *20,000 Leagues*

Under the Sea by Jules Verne. New York: Bantam Books, 1964.

"Beyond 1984." *Playboy,* January 1979, p. 170.

Dandelion Wine. New York: Bantam Books, 1976. Contains Bradbury's autobiographical introduction "Just This Side of Byzantium."

Fahrenheit 451. New York: Ballantine Books, 1953.

The Golden Apples of the Sun. New York: Bantam Books, 1961.

"Gotcha!" *Redbook,* August 1978, p. 95.

The Halloween Tree. New York: Alfred A. Knopf, 1972.

The Illustrated Man. New York: Bantam Books, 1952.

I Sing the Body Electric! New York: Alfred A. Knopf, 1969.

Long after Midnight. New York: Alfred A. Knopf, 1976.

The Machineries of Joy. New York: Bantam Books, 1965.

Mars and the Mind of Man. (with Arthur C. Clarke, Bruce Murray, Carl Sagan, and Walter Sullivan). New York: Harper & Row, 1973. Contains discussions and photographs on some of the most recent discoveries about Mars, which may be compared with the theories of Lowell.

The Martian Chronicles. New York: Bantam Books, 1972. This edition does not have the prefatory note by Clifton Fadiman found in the 1954 edition.

A Medicine for Melancholy. New York: Bantam Books, 1960.

The October Country. New York: Ballantine Books, 1956.

Pillar of Fire and Other Plays. New York: Bantam Books, 1975.

R is for Rocket. New York: Bantam Books, 1976.

S is for Space. New York: Bantam Books, 1976.

The Small Assassin. Frogmore, St. Albans, England: Panther Books, 1976.
    This British paperback contains several stories from *Dark Carnival* not subsequently reprinted in *October Country.* It is available in some of the larger U.S. bookstores.

Something Wicked This Way Comes. New York: Bantam Books, 1963.

"Steiner out of Kong by Cooper." Album notes to the original motion picture score of "King Kong," composed by Max

Steiner. Los Angeles: United Artists Records, UA-LA373-G. 1975.

"A Summer Day." *Redbook,* August 1979, p. 51.

Switch on the Night. New York: Pantheon Books, 1955.

Timeless Stories for Today and Tomorrow. New York: Bantam Books, 1961.

> 26 stories of fantasy by various authors, edited and with an introduction by Bradbury.

The Vintage Bradbury. New York: Vintage Books, 1965. Introduction by Gilbert Highet.

When Elephants Last in the Dooryard Bloomed. New York: Alfred A. Knopf, 1977.

The Wonderful Ice Cream Suit and Other Plays. New York: Bantam Books, 1972.

Zen and the Art of Writing and The Joy of Writing: Two Essays. Santa Barbara, CA.: Capra Press, 1973.

Other Sources

Brackett, Leigh. *The Sword of Rhiannon.* New York: Ace Books, 1953.

Burroughs, Edgar Rice. *A Princess of Mars.* New York: Ballantine Books, 1963.

Čapek, Karel. *R. U. R.* from *R.U.R. and The Insect Play* by the Brothers Čapek. Translated by P. Selver. New York: Oxford University Press, 1961.

Elliot, Jeff. "The Bradbury Chronicles." Interview. *Future,* October 1978, p. 22.

Ellison, Harlan, ed. *Again Dangerous Visions.* New York: New American Library, 1972.

Goldstone, Tony, ed. *The Pulps: Fifty Years of American Pop Culture.* New York: Chelsea House, 1976.

> A good popular history of the sort of magazine in which Bradbury published many of his early stories. Contains the otherwise uncollected story "Wake for the Living," first published in 1947 in *Dime Mystery Magazine.*

Gunn, James. *Alternate Worlds: The Illustrated History of Science Fiction.* Englewood Cliffs, NJ.: Prentice Hall, 1975.

Another good popular history, well-illustrated. Includes many details about writers and editors with whom Bradbury has been associated.

Hamilton, Edith. *Mythology.* New York: New American Library, n. d.

A very readable reference work summarizing many of the Greek, Roman and Norse myths that influenced Bradbury's writing.

Herrigel, Eugen. *Zen in the Art of Archery.* New York: Vintage Books, 1971.

The direct inspiration for Bradbury's essay "Zen and the Art of Writing."

Hoyt, William Graves. *Lowell and Mars.* Tucson: University of Arizona Press, 1976.

Indick, Ben P. "The Drama of Ray Bradbury." N.p.: T-K Graphics, 1977.

A critical essay in pamphlet form. Treats Bradbury's radio, stage and screen plays. Includes a list of published plays. The pamphlet may be located in some science fiction book stores.

Johnson, Wayne L. "The Invasion Stories of Ray Bradbury." In *Critical Encounters: Writers and Themes in Science Fiction,* edited by Dick Riley. New York: Frederick Ungar Publishing Co., 1978.

————. Unpublished interview with Ray Bradbury on October 5, 1978.

Kraus, Maggie, comp. "Tour of the North Branch of the Waukegan River: The Streets that Border the Ravine." Mimeographed. Waukegan, Ill.: Waukegan Historical Society—Heritage Committee Waukegan Bicentennial Commission, n. d.

Lewis, Barbara. "Ray Bradbury, the Martian Chronicler." Interview. *Starlog,* August 1979, p. 28.

Ley, Willy. *Watchers of the Skies: An Informal History of Astronomy from Babylon to the Space Age.* New York: Viking Press, 1963.

Lieberman, Archie. *The Mummies of Guanajuato.* New York: Harry N. Abrams, 1978.

A photographic tour of Guanajuato and of the famous mummies. Bradbury's story "The Next in Line" is included as an introduction.

Lowell, Percival. *Mars As the Abode of Life.* New York: Macmillan Co., 1909.

_____. *Mars and Its Canals.* New York: Macmillan Co., 1907.

Madsen, Axel. *John Huston.* Garden City, N.Y.: Doubleday & Company, 1978.

Contains details of Bradbury's stay in Ireland while working on the screenplay for "Moby Dick."

Meredith, Burgess. "Burgess Meredith Reads Ray Bradbury." Phonograph record. Bergen Field, N.J.: Lively Arts Recording Corp. Lively Arts 30004, n.d.

Dramatic readings by Meredith of "There Will Come Soft Rains" and "Marionettes, Inc."

Mitchell, Lisa. "Ray Bradbury: He Sees the Future—and it Works." *Family Weekly,* 16 July 1978, p. 4.

Naha, Ed. "The Martian Chronicles." *Future Life,* November 1979, p. 18.

Magazine article detailing the filming of Bradbury's book for television.

Nolan, William F. "The Published Books and Stories of Ray Bradbury."

Appendix to *The Martian Chronicles* by Ray Bradbury. Garden City, N. Y.: Doubleday & Company, 1973.

A chronological listing of Bradbury's books and short stories published through 1972.

_____. "Ray Bradbury: A Biographical Sketch." Preface to *The Martian Chronicles* by Ray Bradbury. Garden City, N. Y.: Doubleday & Company, 1973.

_____. *The Ray Bradbury Companion.* Detroit: Bruccoli Clark Books, 1975. Introduction by Bradbury. Contains biographical information, many photographs of Bradbury's family and friends, reproduction of some of Bradbury's manuscripts, information on foreign editions of various works, and other details of Bradbury's work and career.

Rovin, Jeff. *From the Land Beyond Beyond*. New York: Berkeley Windhover Books, 1977.

Contains details of Ray Harryhausen's filsm, including his work on "The Beast from 20,000 Fathoms."

Slusser, George Edgar. *The Ray Bradbury Chronicles*. San Bernardino, CA: Borgo Press, 1977.

Critical essay in booklet form. Concludes with a list of Bradbury's published books.

Truffaut, François. *Hitchcock*. New York: Simon and Schuster, 1967.

Welles, H. G. *The Complete Science Fiction Treasury of H. G. Welles*. New York: Avenel Books, 1978.

Index

Abbreviation used in the Index